UNSTOPPABLE WOMEN WITH ADHD

SIMPLE STRATEGIES TO BUILD RELATIONSHIPS,
REDUCE STRESS, GAIN EFFECTIVE ORGANIZATIONAL
SKILLS TO TRANSFORM CHALLENGES INTO
TRIUMPHS AND RESTORE INNER PEACE

ISABELLE RAY

CONTENTS

PRELUDE

Take a journey with me for a minute. Imagine there's a parade going on outside. Now, picture yourself not only watching the parade, but also being responsible for the whole band.

This is a different kind of band though. This one is a one-man band contraption thing — you know, where the drum is strapped to the person's back. There's a harmonica gadget that connects to the mouth. You'll find cymbals between the knees and a tambourine tied to each foot. Sounds hectic – and who would want to be that band? There's too much going on simultaneously, right?

Well, welcome to life with ADHD, ladies!

But let's take this one step further. Imagine the strap holding the drum keeps breaking no matter how many times you fix it and no matter what is used to fix it.

Okay, before you start hyperventilating at the thought, let's take a breather and dig into this metaphor a bit.

ADHD, or Attention-Deficit/Hyperactivity Disorder, is like being that one-man band. We'll call it a one-woman band, one-man band, and a one-person band in this book. The instruments represent the multitude of tasks and thoughts you juggle daily. There are the chores, your work, your good and bad relationships, and your hobbies even though you might not get them in during the day. All these things stop you from progressing.

And then there's the internal dialogue that goes on in your head every waking moment.

Each of these tasks requires your attention and effort, and the song you are playing in your one-man band only works if you manage to keep them all going.

What's the symbolism for the broken strap? It's the unpredictable nature of ADHD.

Just when you think you've got the beat going and it's going to be a streak of good luck, something slips. A deadline came and went. The name of someone important who could have helped you is nowhere near the tip of your tongue and certainly didn't come out of your mouth. A project you started is half-done and you can't find the motivation to continue it. Something found a way to stop you. The drum crashes to the ground, the music stutters, and you're left scrambling to put it all back together.

EXPECTATIONS ABOUND

As women, the tune we're expected to play in life often includes even more instruments. Society hands us the trumpet of caretaking, the flute of emotional labor, the xylophone of maintaining a perfectly curated home and social life.

Yet, with ADHD, maintaining the rhythm for all these roles can feel as chaotic as a first-time one-woman band performance on a windy day in the city of Chicago.

The reality is, living with ADHD can be and often is a cacophony. It's as if you feel you're offbeat while the rest of the world is marching unified in time.

RECONNECT TO YOUR RESILIENCE

But hey, let's not forget one crucial thing: There's a certain charm to this one-person band. It's unorthodox, out-of-the-box, as unique as a unique selling proposition for sure, and you could say it's a little wild.

And if you've ever seen one of these bands in action, you can't help but notice there's a certain air of resilience in their performance. It's a persisting spirit that keeps the music going no matter what. That resilience is in you, too. And this resilience is related to your unstoppability. There will be more about unstoppability and resilience later.

Just as every band member needs to know how to play their instrument, understanding ADHD is crucial in learning how to keep your music alive, even when the strap breaks. This book is dedicated to doing just that.

Together, we'll explore the unique ways ADHD manifests in women, learn strategies to manage the drum-strap malfunctions, and find ways to laugh and dance along with the tune. The big goal is to keep you unstoppable in your progress, in achieving your dreams, in overcoming roadblocks in your life and your finances, and more. Resilience is like a fierce friend who always stands up for you and allows you an incredible ability to bounce back from whatever life throws you.

Remember this, my ADHD-struggling sisters, the goal isn't to play the parade perfectly. It's to keep marching, keep playing, and make the most beautiful music you can, broken strap and all. After all, the one-man band isn't remarkable because it plays flawlessly. It's remarkable because it keeps going, despite the chaos.

And isn't that a tune we can all dance to?

Now is a good time to stop and chew on these thoughts in between everything else happening in your life today. Thinking of your life in this way is a big paradigm change.

Consider doing your life like that one-woman band with storage houses of resilience that you can draw upon that are built deep into your soul. This type of resilience and unstoppability can be corralled into juggling your career and nurturing your family. With it, you have a remarkable knack for thriving no matter what the adversity is that shows up.

SECRET 1 ABOUT WOMEN WITH ADHD

One of the secrets of life for women with ADHD and of your unstoppability is actually an oxymoron. To stay unstoppable means you stop and smell the roses when a big paradigm change just hit you square in the face. Slow down when you have ADHD? That's the oxymoron.

Yes, the secret is that it's important to slow down and smell the roses in your relationships, finances, career, and your family.

To be unstoppable, you actually have to stop occasionally.

When you stop yourself for a moment, you simply tell yourself to slow down and that you're taking a time out, allowing your soul to catch up with what's happening.

You see, it's easy for us with ADHD to get in our daily mode of go, go, go. Do this, that, and the next thing. Something comes up, let's do that. Forget about the other things. We invest our whole soul in that new thing – temporarily.

But what we are doing is leaving all the loose ends open for all those other projects. And those loose ends interfere with your resilience. We haven't been told that if we have an a-ha moment, we have to integrate it into what's happening in the rest of the parts of our lives.

When a paradigm change hits us, we have two options. We can see that this new idea will be life-changing. But our old way of doing things is to say, "Yeah, that's a big deal..." and keep on plugging away at everything else. We tend to dishonor its importance.

And that ends up leaving us feeling fragmented later on, affecting our resilience. All those other projects never receive the benefit of the new idea that's been presented.

The one big secret is to integrate what our soul is experiencing with the rest of the parts of us that are running on the maze wheel. We have to speak to them and say, "Hey Straight A student inside me, we've had a revelation. It's ... and it's going to give us an upgrade in how we approach studying... Hey, Ms. Mom, new data came in and it's gonna help you multi-task from now on... Hey Sexy Lady, something happened that is going to make you sexier..."

This integration only takes a few minutes, but boy is it powerful. I learned this the hard way by just pressing through life and never emotionally integrating new things. And what I found was that the integration concept didn't seem to appear to matter in the short-term, but it certainly did in the long term. Ten years later, I looked back and couldn't see my progress or the patterns that had propelled me to where I was. I was at a loss for which way to go. I was stopped in my forward momentum because my soul lacked this input.

Now after doing this emotional integration at least weekly, I'm much more stable in who I am. When others say negative things to me, it's easy to brush off the comments quickly with few side effects. I stay solid in who I am. I'm able to bring out the creative person I am and accomplish multiple things.

And when I look back at my own character development, I see I'm a lot nicer to myself. There's a lot less negative self-talk when something didn't get done. I realize the task just didn't get done yet. That task will have its day and time to be completed and I assign it to the future. My resilience has reared up and I make progress, just as you will.

So for this book, I'm going to continue to point out more of these 'global' things that have affected the lives of others and myself with ADHD. I'll show you that when you deal with the overall patterns in your life and in your soul, things have a way of coming together into that beautiful music a lot faster and easier.

This is just one of the keys. This book will be full of more of them so you'll be able to manage your situation more effectively. You'll be able to reduce stress levels. You'll be able to stay organized and on task. And you will find that your relationships – both with yourself and others will become more meaningful.

You see, I believe that all of us women with ADHD have some core things in common. And the one thing that we all need is a bit of help from others.

Sure, you can have friends that help out but living day to day with them often seems painstakingly slow. You all deal with situations one by one and literally several of the situations drag out over a long time frame. They become boring to you after a while. "What? She's still talking about that? Let's move on" is a thought in your mind. And that can lead to friendship conflict and breakdown in the near future.

When you can get a lot of these brain patterns figured out simultaneously over a few weeks instead of 10 or 20 years, you're in seventh heaven as an ADHD prodigy with the world at your fingertips.

And that's where we women were meant to be, right?

INTRODUCTION

You are unique. You already know that. Every human is as unique as every snowflake.

But you are more unique than how you picture yourself. As a woman with ADHD, your life will be more impressive than many non-ADHD friends. There are things you will go through that they'll never have to go through. And these challenges will be fostering your unstoppability.

And by the way, there are two different terms that you will come across on the internet: neurodiverse and neurotypical. Neurodiverse is everyone who doesn't think like the rest of the "normal" population. Neurodiverse is a term for you with ADHD.

Neurotypical is the "normal" population. Neurotypical is "them," those who don't have ADHD.

The "neuro" part of these words refers to the brain. Thus, because you have ADHD – and scientists have confirmed that your brain is wired differently, you are neurodiverse. You think in diverse ways that others don't even consider.

Neurotypical people are regular, everyday people whose brains are not wired differently from the norm and what is expected scientifically to happen in humans.

WHEN DID ADHD BEGIN?

Everything may have seemed remarkable for many of your early years – until puberty. When that hit, ADHD symptoms seemed to have hit you. Think back to your own life and see if this is true.

Those ADHD symptoms were different from what boys experience with ADHD.

The truth is that women experience ADHD differently than boys and men.

Below is a list of four ways ADHD shows itself differently:

1. Inattentiveness and sometimes hyperactivity

2. In college, women with ADHD rise to the life of the party position. However, there's a gnawing inside them about all the homework they haven't done or all the friends and family members they haven't connected with.

3. People don't believe you have ADHD when you tell them. So whatever you tell them, you can't explain why you forgot this or that. They won't buy it.

4. Girls with ADHD have symptoms that go undiagnosed or misdiagnosed.

In your early years, you may have learned that your inattentiveness was a character flaw. It put a 'mark' on you that was similar to being in the line of girls at school who were the ones never chosen to be on the team with the athletic girls. These little hits gave you jabs of rejection that you couldn't overlook and became an open wound in your soul.

In reality, we can't expect other girls our age or even our teachers and authority figures in our lives to be up to date with every type of medical condition. They didn't know how unique you were or why your focus seemed to falter.

Did your life go in the direction of these four manifestations of ADHD for women?

WHY YOUR ADHD WASN'T DISCOVERED YEARS AGO

The fact is that symptoms of women with ADHD are likely to go undiagnosed or they will be misdiagnosed. ADHD looks different in girls than in boys. And until there's a massive re-education process and awareness campaigns on this, it's likely to continue.

Inattentiveness can masquerade itself as poor concentration to those who didn't receive the information from the awareness campaign. Inattentiveness can also look like you're incapable of organizing tasks.

This often ends up leading to confusion, frustration, and isolation. And these feelings will definitely stop you and your progress forward in life. Moreover, they can leave you down in the dumps and suppress your resilience.

DON'T STAY LOW IN BLAME!

Not completing tasks you know you have to do brings guilt and anxiety. Dealing with this guilt is imperative because otherwise, it will pile up until it's overwhelming.

But as a 13-year-old, who taught you how to deal with guilt or anxiety? The answer may have been given to you in the form of a medication, which stuffed your feelings into a bigger and bigger suitcase every year.

And when you tell people you have ADHD, and they don't believe you, that's dishonoring you and your opinion. It may even fall under the label of gaslighting, telling you that what you are feeling – and your reality – is not valid. Without realizing it, they were calling you a liar. And no one wants to – or should have to prove she's not a liar – unless there's a crime involved.

All those years you were undiagnosed or misdiagnosed have led to confusion that still sits inside your brain. So, in the one-woman band, you have another instrument to juggle – confusion and all the other negative emotions.

Your struggle has been confirmed. Your challenges are actual. And there are specific ways to deal with the remainders of gaslighting and stuffing feelings. Answers will be provided in this book.

SUCCESS WILL COME TO YOU DESPITE ADHD

One more thing that is true is that you really and truly can live a meaningful and successful life. It's not impossible. It's probable if you learn how this whole picture of women with ADHD works and use it to your advantage.

This is similar to giving you the cheat sheet for all the questions you would be asked on an exam. Or if that advantage causes you some guilt … think of being given an ADHD guardian angel who will walk with you your whole life, tipping you off to this and that. That may seem like a fairer advantage since most people believe they already have a guardian angel.

Yes, sometimes we all need a little bit of help – and the thing is that if we look around in our environment, that support is actually there right in front of us. We didn't recognize it.

This book can help you.

You'll learn:

- how to manage what's going on in your life more effectively.
- how to reduce stress levels by converting them into opportunities. It's an immediate way to relax. You'll be amazed.
- how to stay organized and on task. Who doesn't need this?

And best of all, you'll learn how to develop a better relationship with yourself and others around you.

This book provides simple and practical strategies to help you take control of your life and truly become unstoppable. You can use the disorder you feel right now as one of the most significant advantages in your life.

Imagine what life will be like when you are playing the flute at work, the cymbals at home, the harmonica at school, and the bagpipes when you're out in public – and when you do it so effortlessly that people stop and say, "How does she do it? How does she balance them all so perfectly when it seems so impossible? And how does the music always sound so soothing, yet stimulative, so right on time, and make me want to come back and hear more?"

They hang around you. They start to dance. You bring out the best part of them. You make them laugh and cheer without trying. You're doing exactly what you were meant to do in your life. You're right on track.

And you're proud of what you have accomplished. You know there's more to come. You love life and being the one-woman band. Nothing scares you. Nothing makes you anxious. No one can gaslight you anymore. You take on the challenges of life with gusto, knowing your resilience will mount up and help you through it.

You're a master of your destiny.

With the proper support, you can learn to manage your ADHD effectively to create a future filled with success and fulfillment.

And more than that, you can and will become unstoppable.

WHAT DOES IT MEAN TO BE UNSTOPPABLE?

Being unstoppable is a phrase that means you possess incredible determination and unwavering resolve that is relentless in the pursuit of your goals and aspirations. This determination is there regardless of the challenges, obstacles, or setbacks.

Can you see that it's a mindset? When you take an unstoppable stance, you refuse to let difficulties distract you from your commitment to move forward. The commitments and responsibilities could be for anything – a degree, a job or promotion, starting a family, getting through family issues, learning different skills, or even deepening your relationship with God.

Someone who is unstoppable has courage and resilience, and it's palpable to others. It's what makes someone a great leader. Yes, if you have ADHD, you've been given the perfect opportunity to become a leader who makes a difference in life, something that many who are neurotypical don't have till much later in life.

Someone who is unstoppable also has an unshakable belief in themselves, giving them the energy to take that inner fire that will help them achieve, grow, and change positively.

Being unstoppable doesn't mean mistakes are not made. Plenty of failures and adversity are in the path of someone unstoppable. But that's the thing – failures and adversity are in the way so an invincible person faces them head-on, learning from them. Every failure and every adversity is a stepping stone on the path to success – and resilience.

Once you reframe your walk with ADHD through life to an unstoppable one where you are playing the music of that one-woman band in a harmonious melody, a prominent inner change occurs within the recesses of your brain. The idea resets everything for you. And it's like you have stumbled upon a hidden gold nugget worth millions.

Your brain begins to have revelations more often, and these revelations decipher the intricate patterns of your thoughts and behaviors.

Right now, you may have found that living with ADHD makes you feel like you have to navigate life's challenges in a void without help from anyone else. Others can't possibly understand what you're going through.

But now, you can pull out the "unstoppable" and "one-woman band producing pleasant melodies" cards when faced with new challenges and tell your brain to find the answer. When you do, it's as if you have stepped into the shoes of a commander. What you are controlling is this beautiful brain that you have. You're becoming more familiar with how it wants to work and directing it to go in the way you want and need it to go.

The "unstoppable" and "one-woman band producing pleasant melodies" cards give your brain direction. In contrast, in the past, there was none. These cards tell your brain to provide an idea or behavior that fits a challenging situation. Still, these cards have to produce a great result. If you used only the unstoppable card, you would get good and bad solutions. But using both of them, your success can soar.

This book is about helping you become unstoppable to turn life's roadblocks into stepping stones toward your aspirations. For example, you will read a chapter on impulsivity. Your mind grasps the information about the topic and how it relates to those with ADHD.

Then, a situation arises where impulsivity could be your choice. Still, with this new reframe, there's a pause – even just for a split second, and in that split second, your brain has found a unique solution that doesn't allow you to proceed forward on that path. You, the one-woman band are now producing a pleasant, excellent melody.

The same thing can happen for hyperfocus, which you'll learn about in one of the latter chapters of this book. With the information learned on the topic, you recognize that your ability to hyperfocus can lead to incredible bursts of creativity and productivity. Who doesn't want that?

Yes, it means that you do a trade-off of your time for it – and that's okay... but because you learned how hyperfocus works, you know the downside can put you in a time warp where you neglect other people and neglect your own health. You make a better choice and your life changes, little by little.

MOVING FORWARD INTO BOLD DECISIONS

This new reframe of being unstoppable and a one-woman band producing pleasant melodies have given your brain additional information to draw upon for your answers. When you hyperfocus, you turn it into being "in the zone" or at least address all the things that still need to be addressed when you are in deep thought, such as your health and those around you.

This new reframe directs you towards bold decisions and courageous leaps into what you would have considered the unknown, but now the results are different. Now those leaps are only going in one direction because you directed them. There's a lot less relationship and situational fallout you don't have to deal with. You're making better choices.

The self-belief you build from knowing how ADHD brains work will transcend the self-doubt that often accompanies ADHD. It allows you to set goals that resonate with your passions and strengths. You can pursue them with a determination that you didn't fully realize you possessed previously.

VICTORIES AND CARVING OUT YOUR INDIVIDUALITY

Embracing unstoppability within the context of ADHD means accepting that your path will not look like everyone else's, and that's okay. This is how you carve out your extraordinary individuality that the world is waiting to experience. There are still challenges ahead, but there are more victories because each challenge brings multiple wins. With every step you take toward your goals, you recognize the strength of your spirit and the untapped, unstoppable potential within you.

This journey of self-discovery and embracing your own unstoppability is continuous, marked by moments of growth, learning, and self-compassion. Living with ADHD has put you on this journey long before others experience the same challenge. In fact, some people never seem to embrace a similar journey. And the difference between someone who embraces it and someone who doesn't is vast. It's as if those who don't take the opportunity end up staying the same as they were in grammar school or high school, even though they are now in their 50s and 60s!

Maybe you are in your 50s or 60s right now – and that's okay. For you, the choices that are available now to make this journey work to your advantage were not known before. Those earlier decades in your life have been marked with battle scars. But that doesn't mean that the reframe of the unstoppable and one-woman band playing a pleasant melody doesn't still hold true. They do – and you will see results.

This journey you are on takes the complexities of living with ADHD one by one and acknowledges the remarkable strengths that come with it. As you continue along this path, you'll be excited to see how the unique qualities inside you shape the narrative of your life in ways you never imagined possible.

And you won't have to spend 40 years to have success!

This book will help you navigate the journey and provide the tools to find joy, self-love, and acceptance.

The big words for today are:

- Possibility becomes probability.
- Uniqueness must be celebrated.
- Step into your future now. Why wait?
- Be the one-woman band you were meant to be.
- UNSTOPPABLE!
- The one-person band is producing pleasant melodies!

As you may already see, this book was written just for you. Your timing is perfect. All those challenges you have faced in the past will be placed into a new perspective that brings success to fruition day by day!

It may be time for another break… is all this a paradigm change for you? It certainly was for me many years ago.

Join me for some hot chocolate or tea.

Then go on out and make some great music today!

1

ALL ABOUT ADHD

Knowledge is power, and one of the best things you can do is learn all the innuendos about ADHD and ADHD in women.

What this knowledge does for you is impactful! Let's say you're in a situation where you just missed a deadline at work. You can clearly see that it was your fault.

Someone with no knowledge of ADHD would react this way:

- Blame themselves.
- Start the negative self-talk.
- Ramp it up, and by the time they get home from work, they are agitated.

Hopefully, nobody or no pet is around to kick or tear down with words.

What they don't realize is their negativity affects their ability to be resilient and to be unstoppable.

On the other hand, someone who has knowledge about ADHD reacts differently. Her thought process may go like this:

- "Hmm... I see this is definitely my fault (self-responsibility)."
- "I must evaluate the choices that led to this moment and what I could do differently."
- "I need to think about the consequences and how they could affect me and realize my choices and consequences go hand in hand."
- "I will do this with the aid of my partner (or best friend), who can help me see something new about myself."

There's no negative self-talk in this example. The responses are pro-active.

Your body 'hears' what you are saying and thinking. Then, it acts accordingly. It's not uncommon that negative self-talk leads to diseases such as cancer, autoimmune diseases, and even "mysterious" diseases that doctors can't solve.

So, part of being nice to yourself is to start catching yourself when you start down the path of negative self-talk. "Cancel, cancel that thought" is how you can reverse something that sneaks into your consciousness. Personally, I package up the thought and throw it in the trash mentally.

With this in mind, let's move forward to find out what ADHD is and the different types of ADHD.

WHAT IS ADHD? WHO HAS ADHD?

ADHD stands for Attention-deficit / hyperactivity disorder. It is considered a neurodevelopmental disorder of childhood. As the brain and nervous system develop in childhood, some changes occur in how the child's brain is wired about daily functioning, interpersonal relationships, studying and achieving accomplishments, and more.

The child's brain isn't functioning like 'normal' children (neuotypicals) – but this does not mean it is not working! Scientists have found that the networks of nerves in the brain regarding reward and planning associated with focus, attention, movement, and switching attention between tasks behave differently in those with ADHD. Also, dopamine and norepinephrine levels appear to be lower in those with ADHD.

Prenatal Roots?

It's even possible that the roots of ADHD started prenatally. Alcohol or tobacco use during pregnancy could have set up a child's brain for the condition. However, the studies on alcohol are mixed. One meta-study evaluated different alcohol consumption levels women consumed before birth and checked for ADHD in the children born after that. They found no increased risk of ADHD symptoms in children born to moms who drank less than 70 grams of alcohol per week.

However, verbal comprehension and cognitive reasoning in children were found to be significantly different in children whose moms had a heavy alcohol intake during pregnancy compared to controls. The study occurred at San Diego University and was reported in the journal Neuropsychology in 2013.

Other studies confirm that heavy drinking during pregnancy can and does produce developmental defects. For example, prenatal and postnatal growth retardation and central nervous system dysfunction are consequences of fetal alcohol exposure. There are also facial anomalies. The central nervous system dysfunction includes mental retardation, hyperactivity, sleep disorders, and behavioral difficulties.

Premature birth or low birth weight have also been associated with ADHD. But in 2017, Australian researchers commented in the journal Current Psychiatry Reports that "None of the proposed prenatal risk factors can be confirmed as causal for ADHD, and the stronger the study design, the less likely it is to support an association."

So, nothing was etched in stone for prenatal factors in 2017.

Then, in 2018, a report published on the meta-study of 12 different studies showed that very preterm/very low birth weight and extremely preterm / extremely low birth weight infants have a higher risk for ADHD, 3 times higher than controls. The more extreme the cases, the higher the odds ratio.

The same researchers from Brazil and Turkey universities drew data from 29 studies with 3,504 subjects related to ADHD symptomatology. They found significant associations with inattention, hyperactivity, impulsivity, and combined symptoms compared to controls.

If prenatal factors affected you, it's entirely possible that they put forth a block to your resilience even before you saw the light of day.

AN EXAMPLE OF HOW THE BRAIN IS DIFFERENT IN ADHD

A boy with ADHD is more impulsive than a neurotypical boy. This means when an idea comes into the brain of someone with ADHD, he proceeds forward and acts upon it rather than thinking about whether or not that idea is good enough to move forward with.

The parts of the brain that spend time thinking about whether or not to proceed with an idea are called executive functions. They are located primarily in the prefrontal cortex. They include planning, considering the positives and negatives of a situation, looking ahead to the future, and considering what might happen due to a choice. The frontal lobe, in particular, is responsible for perceiving time, judgment, language, planning, emotional regulation, and delaying gratification.

Is the Brain Physically Different?

Children with ADHD have been found to have a small frontal lobe. This area may take a more extended amount of time to develop in a particular child. If so, one can expect that the symptoms lessen as the child matures. In many cases, signs of ADHD decline with age.

HOW DO GIRLS PRESENT WITH ADHD?

For girls, symptoms are all about inattention rather than hyperactivity. Although every child will have moments of inattention since learning to focus comes with age, a girl with ADHD will experience them more frequently. Studies have shown that for those with ADHD, when they try to concentrate, their prefrontal cortex receives less blood flow, making it more challenging to focus.

THE GOOD PART ABOUT ADHD

When learning about ADHD, it's essential to hold a space open in your mind that some good is there for ADHD. It's not all bad. This is true for any disease. Looking for something good to occur prevents despondency and brings hope. It keeps you on the track to move forward in the direction you are supposed to go. It contributes to your resilience and unstoppability.

There actually is a good part about ADHD. You see, all this inattentiveness isn't happening 24/7 in the mind of a girl with ADHD. And the inattentiveness is not equitable with stupidity! The truth is that there are some things that she LOVES doing. And when she does them, she is focusing on them and heavy in thought about them. All this focus builds many parts of her brain. And the result is that she will soon show the world that she excels at certain things.

You could say that in many cases, the brain of a girl or boy with ADHD functions BETTER than a child without ADHD. And the beauty of all this is that these built-up areas of the brain are treasures that the child will discover on her own. Maybe she's the next great poet, artist, or writer. Perhaps she's the next mathematician who is better than Einstein. Maybe she's the next community development leader better than Gandhi!

So if you have been told that ADHD will ruin your life, it will prevent you from finding a good man, it will keep you in the poorhouse, or other lies, set them onto a scrap pile right now in your mind and light a fire to them. Whoever told you them was operating out of the lies told to them – and not seeing the beauty in you. It's there. Will you let that beauty come out now?

WHY WASN'T I DIAGNOSED EARLIER IN LIFE? WHY DID I SUFFER SO LONG?

Let's talk about how many people are just like you. It is estimated that if you have ADHD, you aren't alone. About 9.4% of children have it, and the National Institute of Mental Health has found that 5.4% of adult men and 3.2% of adults have ADD/ADHD.

Let's see what this number really means. There are 74 million children in the U.S.; if 9.4% of children have ADHD, that's almost 7 million other children. Seven million other children have brains experiencing the same things you are experiencing.

There are 105 boys born for every 100 girls. With 38.85 million boys in the U.S., 3.65 million boys have ADHD. There are 35.15 million girls, and assuming the rate is the same – 9.4%, there are 3.3 million girls with ADHD.

If the number of girls in every state was the same – although it's not – there would be 66,000 girls in your state who have ADHD, just like you. That gives you a lot of potential friends!

In 2022, psychologists from the University of California at Berkeley and San Francisco concluded that girls meet diagnostic criteria for ADHD at just under half the rates of boys. That number becomes much closer to equal by adulthood.

Most cases of ADHD in girls are diagnosed around age 12, much later than when it's diagnosed in boys. Boys may be diagnosed from age 4 and up. That's because their hyperactivity and impulsivity can't be ignored. In girls, their inattentiveness is more subtle and needs a trained eye to find.

There are many cases where ADHD in girls is not diagnosed until adulthood. Yikes! I'm already sad about that because they probably have built up some severe scar tissue around their heart from what's been happening to them.

ADHD is not usually diagnosed until behavior problems arise and disrupt a classroom or a family. The behavior problems become the red flags that something is wrong. It's easy for teachers in a classroom to consider the symptoms of ADHD as being defiant or unable to understand instructions given to her.

However, any teacher who believes this – or worse yet, is telling you that you are defiant or not so bright is not telling the truth! In a way, we can't blame the teacher because there's obviously a lack of knowledge in the situation. Still, nevertheless, this idea is harming you. More about healing from that later...

LET'S COMPLETE THE PICTURE EVEN MORE

There are some other statistics you should know.

- A 2016 Centers for Disease Control and Prevention (CDC) study broke down the number of people with ADHD in the U.S. even further. They found that between the ages of 2 and 5, there are 388,000 children with ADHD, which is 2.4% of the population. Between ages 6 and 11, there are 2.4 million children with ADHD (9.6% of the population). And between ages 12 and 17, there are 3.3 million adolescents with ADHD.
- A 2020 study estimated that in adults, both male and female, the percentage of those with ADHD is 2.8 percent. In the U.S., that number is 0.96%, according to another study in 2019. However, prior studies have stated a 5.4% diagnosis rate in men compared to 3.2% in women in the U.S. population.
- The number of children with ADHD is rising in the U.S., estimated at 11% in 2011, compared to 7.8% in 2003.

- Of the children in the U.S. with ADHD, about a third of them take ADHD medication only, and another third takes medication and participates in behavioral therapies. Only about 15% use behavioral treatment without a prescription.
- About 62% of ADHD children are currently on ADHD medications. This is broken down into only 18% of 2 to 5-year-olds, 68.6% of those between ages 6 and 11, and 62.1% between ages 12 to 17.
- Children diagnosed with ADHD are likelier to have a binge eating disorder called Loss of Control Eating Syndrome. That number is 12 times more likely!
- It's common for those with ADHD to have a co-existing condition. Only 1.2% have Tourette syndrome, which makes sense because the disease is uncommon. About 14% have been diagnosed with autism spectrum disorder, 17% with depression, 33% with anxiety, 45% with a learning disorder, and 52% with behavioral or conduct problems.
- Diagnoses of ADHD in adults are proliferating - now, the incidence is four times higher than children's diagnoses. Children have a 26.4% increase in ADHD diagnoses, while adults have a 123.3% increase.

WHAT ARE THE DIFFERENT TYPES OF ADHD?

Let's dig into the next level of ADHD. Ready for more?

There are three different categories of ADHD:

1. Predominantly inattentive
2. Predominantly hyperactive or impulsive
3. Both #1 and #2

Inattentive Type

When a girl (or boy) is predominantly inattentive, different possible types of behavior reflect this label. These symptoms below tell everyone that the child likely has the predominantly inattentive type of ADHD.

Here's the list:

- Easily distracted
- Trouble staying focused
- Disorganized
- Look like they are unmotivated or apathetic
- Tired, sluggish, or moving slowly
- Spacey or preoccupied
- Forgetfulness
- Poor follow-through
- Trouble listening when others talk to them
- Tendency to lose things
- Complaints of being bored

- Time is not managed well

If a child under the age of 17 has six of these, a diagnosis of ADHD is given. For anyone over 17, the diagnosis is made with five of the characteristics. These types of behaviors must occur frequently and cannot be occasional. They also must be present continuously for at least six months and should appear in at least two settings (home, school, or work).

Who said so is usually the next question to answer. Well, who said so is the textbook for how psychiatrists diagnose ADHD. It's called the DSM-V. That's the bible for diagnosing ADHD.

Hyperactive or Impulsive ADHD

Now, in this hyperactive or impulsive ADHD category, you will have symptoms and behaviors other than what was seen in the inattentive type.

Hyperactivity means excessive activity. The child is simply moving too much. That movement may appear as fidgeting around in one's seat, having too much energy, unable to sit still, or by being talkative. Being impulsive means making choices without thinking about consequences.

Here are additional symptoms of hyperactivity:

- Squirming in the chair, tapping hands and/or feet, or fidgeting with hands
- Cannot stay seated in a classroom or at work
- Talks too much
- Can't wait for their turn
- Interrupts others in a conversation or does not respect other people's things and uses them without permission. Older adolescents and adults may decide to take over a situation.
- Plays loudly. When participating in leisure activities, the child is loud.
- Wants to cut into conversations, finish people's sentences, or the teacher can't get the question out before the child blurts the answer out loud.
- Always wound up or on the go
- Runs or climbs in places where these are not allowed.

The goal is to count all the ones that apply to you or the child in question. This category is scored similarly to the inattentive category. There are nine possible behaviors, and if the score is five, then there's a diagnosis of ADHD for an adolescent over 17. A score of six is needed for a child under 17.

Feel free to check off any on the lists so far! Get your score!

Combined Type

Someone may check off symptoms or behaviors from BOTH categories. If this happens, the diagnosis will be the Combined Type.

Now, this is all pretty straightforward so far.

Let's get into more detail on the diagnosis of ADHD from the doctor's point of view. It would help if you understood what's happening in his head, too.

ALL ABOUT THE DIAGNOSIS OF ADHD

Children or adults are diagnosed with ADHD by doctors and mental health providers.

The diagnosis is made based on the criteria in the DSM-5-TR textbook. But there's a potential problem with this way of doing things. That textbook ADHD diagnosis was created after only testing children between the ages of 4 and 17.

What! How accurate could it be for me if I'm in my 30s? This is what you may be thinking. Well, after age 17, the doctor has to think outside the box. In this case, he may use a person's history and intuition to determine whether or not someone older than 17 really has ADHD.

Other doctors have used continuous performance tests that monitor for attention and impulsivity. Once a doctor sees a pattern, he will most likely give the diagnosis.

And other doctors use a brain scan to help them decide.

So it's not like the doctors decide randomly who gets the diagnosis and who doesn't!

HOW DOES THE DIAGNOSTIC PROCESS START?

The next important thing to know is what happens first, second, third, etc. to get a diagnosis.

You'll likely start with your primary care physician to get a diagnosis. That's good because most people like their primary care physician. However, you need a specialist for the diagnosis. Either your primary care physician is skilled in this, or he's not. Black and white. Skill doesn't depend on whether you like the person or not.

If your doctor is in the gray zone, here's what to do when he says he can diagnose ADHD: Ask how long it will take. He says oh, about 45 minutes.

This answer shoved him to the black zone of the black-and-white scale, where white means he's the white coat that can do the job, and black means he can't.

The answer he gave was wrong because there's a lot more that's involved in this process. Your discussion with him is not over yet. You want to be sure that you're both on the same page and that his answers mean what you are thinking.

Ask him what type of assessments he'll do during those 45 minutes. If he says he can determine it by talking to you, he's clearly not the right doctor for this. You see, specific assessment tests are done in the field to get an accurate diagnosis.

It helps tremendously if you had a specialist. A diagnosis like this affects many things in you – or your child's life. That's why you want it done in the most thorough way possible. It helps if you had someone who does these types of diagnoses all day long, five days a week. The health practitioner who makes the diagnosis should have already diagnosed a minimum of 100 other people with ADHD in their career. So, make sure you ask how many people have been diagnosed.

The potential problem is that a doctor who means well but is incompetent at diagnosing ADHD may be diagnosing the whole neighborhood! That's why you want to make sure he's doing what he should, compared to what other people in the field are doing to determine whether or not you have ADHD. Be discerning! Now you know how.

WHAT IF MY INSURANCE HAS NO EXPERT?

Your health insurance plan may not have an ADHD expert to send you to. If this is the case with your provider, consider going outside your network. Yes, you may need to pay out of your pocket, but you want a pro. Remember, the stakes are high. This is a diagnosis that will affect you for a long time.

Ask your provider what services are available within your network so you'll know what's available after you get the diagnosis elsewhere. It's good to see if you'll also have to make additional payments later. You don't want this to be a surprise!

Going outside the network doesn't have to mean that it will take you hours to find an ADHD expert. The National Alliance on Mental Illness is an excellent resource for professionals in this area.

You can also check with your friends who have children in school. They're the most likely to know someone who went through a similar search – and found the answer.

Here's how to discern their answers: Listen closely to how they recommend someone for this task. Do they say – here's the name of someone – and that's it? If so, that's not good enough. You want someone to spend at least three minutes telling you what it was like, praising the person's work, and more.

When someone is pleased with a professional, they'll bring up things like what happened, how the professional treated them, etc. You want to hear this type of input.

When someone is unhappy with a professional, all they'll give you is their name and number and maybe make one simple statement. They may not want to tarnish another person's character, so they'll shut up after that. You could ask, "Tell me more..." and see what they say. But whatever they say, discern it by asking yourself if this is something that someone would say if they respected the person's services or not.

WHAT TYPES OF HEALTH PROFESSIONALS DO THESE CONSULTATIONS?

The types of health professionals who may be qualified to do this type of consultation are those with specific training – and experience in it.

Your primary care physician may be one of them. However, some of the more likely choices are a psychiatrist, clinical psychologist, neurologist, and clinical social worker.

HOW ELSE CAN I PREPARE FOR THIS CONSULTATION?

The big key is to know and understand ADHD and how the whole consultation process works.

You'll have to do your homework before the initial consultation. The diagnosis has to be met by specific criteria. Part of the homework is knowing the criteria. They include the correct number of symptoms for the diagnosis, the time frame of the symptoms, and the locations in the brain where the person's functioning is impaired.

Expect the doctor to call upon other health professionals (or refer you) for the assessments. For example, vision, hearing, speech, and neurology specialists may contribute their reviews to the mental health professional.

Here's an example of why you need other health professionals involved: Let's say someone has an auditory processing disorder. This means that when this person hears sounds in the room, such as a teacher talking, the sounds are distorted. As a result, they end up checking off many of the same symptoms on the list! So, how does a doctor know the difference between an auditory processing disorder and ADHD? He calls the expert and asks for an assessment.

A complete psychiatric evaluation is also necessary. That's because many of the symptoms of ADHD occur in other health conditions, such as head injuries, thyroid abnormalities, substance use, medication side effects, mood or learning disorders, anxiety, or even other mental health disorders.

Get the picture? So don't take offense when the doctor asks you to visit another health professional for an assessment. He's being diligent and wants to get you a correct diagnosis.

WHAT QUESTIONS WILL I BE ASKED AT THE CONSULTATION?

During the initial diagnostic interview, you'll be asked many questions. You may even feel like you're being interrogated! But calm down ... the doctor wants to know the whole scope of the problem you are experiencing.

Some questions include how long you have had the symptoms and how they affect your quality of life? The doctor is also looking for valuable input from parents and caregivers. And, of course, if the diagnosis is for a child, that child will be talked to plus observed before a diagnosis is made.

SEVERITY OF ADHD

Part of the diagnosis has to include how severe the ADHD is.

This helps direct health professionals toward proper treatment. Health professionals will diagnose the condition as mild, moderate, or severe. There are only three options.

If ADHD is mild, treatment may not be needed. A mild diagnosis means only minor impairment in school, work, or social settings.

A severe diagnosis is made when a higher number of behaviors are seen than what is needed for a diagnosis.

Several behaviors are considered extreme and may cause severe impairment in school, work, home, or social settings.

A moderate diagnosis is when the symptoms or impairment are between mild and severe.

Of course, some cases don't fit precisely into the "box" of diagnosis. Maybe they don't have six symptoms in a category, but a few symptoms are very severe. That's when a clinician may still diagnose that child with ADHD.

WILL THERE BE ANY BLOOD TESTS?

There are no specific blood tests or routine imaging for a diagnosis of ADHD that is considered standard medical practice. However, one psychiatrist, Daniel Amen, M.D., has found that a SPECT scan of the brain can give immense insight into what is really happening in the brain and rule out many different causes of brain abnormalities. That's important because some medical conditions can mimic ADHD.

According to Dr. Amen, SPECT scans were created to help psychiatrists determine what to do for different brain conditions instead of just "guessing" what is wrong with someone.

SPECT scans tell the doctor which parts of the brain have too much activity, too little activity, or healthy activity. A stroke, Alzheimer's, or a traumatic brain injury, drug abuse, and other medical conditions show areas that look like holes in the brain tissue. Even from years ago, a fall or blow to the head shows up on this type of exam.

"Psychiatrists make diagnoses like they did in 1840 when Abe Lincoln was depressed by talking to people and looking for symptom clusters. Imaging showed us that there was a better way. Psychiatrists are the only medical specialists that never look at the organ they treat...Psychiatrists guess," he said in a TEDx Talk.

You may want to watch that TEDx talk – check it out in the references section. You'll be amazed to see the brain scan of a teenage girl with ADHD who was cutting herself, failing in school, and fighting with her parents. She went from Ds and Fs to As and Bs when her brain was balanced with the treatment plan created by the doctors using information from the SPECT scan.

Dr. Amen went against standard medical protocol to start doing SPECT scans. He has done over 250,000 brain scans to date. We'll explain more about his work later in the book. But for now, I want you to know that there are always ways to surpass what is currently done in standard medicine. This is always important, whether it's ADHD, diabetes care, wound care, or other types of care. The bottom line is you want success. You don't want to live with something for the rest of your life if you don't have to. You want to be healed.

We live in a decade of massive technological advancements. And according to Dr. Amen, you are not stuck with the brain you have. You can always make changes for the better in memory, behavior, blood flow, and more.

DIFFERENCE BETWEEN MEN AND WOMEN WITH ADHD

ADHD is three times more common in males than females. Earlier studies have focused on boys, and it wasn't until 2018 and beyond that scientists included girls in their studies. The significant difference is that boys have more serious impulsivity symptoms, while girls have more inattention problems. This was mentioned before. But let's take it deeper.

Boys with ADHD are also more likely to misuse substances and tend to have conduct or antisocial personality disorders. These are called externalization behaviors. These are occurring to an extent because of how the brain works. Some areas have too much activity, while others have too little activity.

Girls with ADHD are more likely to take things personally, internalize them, and tend to have more anxiety, depression, bulimia, and somatic symptom disorders. Girls are more likely to be diagnosed with ADHD if they have personality or internalizing disorders.

Hormonal imbalances can worsen ADHD symptoms in females, and the problem with this is that it may delay diagnosis.

Girls may cope better with ADHD because they tend to develop strategies that deal with any difficulties related to how their brains work.

Some health professionals are suggesting changes be made to how girls are diagnosed. They believe that girls should have more emotional or behavioral problems added to the list to be diagnosed with ADHD.

And there's also some talk that parents overrate symptoms in boys but underestimate symptoms in girls. This is brought up just so you know it; it's not usable when you're in the doctor's office!

But it does give us a clue that maybe you weren't diagnosed a while ago because parents – who aren't trained in any of this – chalked up some of your symptoms to other things. They personally gave you a higher rating on the best person of the year scale and tended to see you like this all year long.

REFLECTIONS

On that note, let's stop here for this chapter. We'll continue it in the next chapter, okay? Don't you feel like it's time to take a break?

So far, you've learned a lot about ADHD. You know what it takes to get a diagnosis, who makes the diagnosis, how to discern whether or not a health professional is suitable for the job, how boys are different than girls when it comes to ADHD, what may have set you on the track to have ADHD and all the symptoms that go with the types and subtypes. That's plenty for now!

I want you to always end each chapter with hope and encouragement and relate it to your resilience and ability to become unstoppable. Remember, you have plenty of other friends out there – ones you don't know right now – neurodiverse friends who have ADHD. You might hook up with them tomorrow; who knows? Friends help you stay resilient. Asking many questions about the process of getting a diagnosis keeps you resilient because until you get answers to them, there will be hesitancy. And hesitancy impedes your unstoppability.

There's a lot of hope on your horizon. Think about what the ADHD brain looks like on imaging with Dr. Amen (did you watch the Youtube video yet?) and how he has helped people with far worse conditions of the brain than ADHD. As he has shown us, those who did not know what was happening in their brain were subject to chaos and tossed around from doctor to doctor.

And frankly, this set them up for a tailspin, not forward progress. Once they knew what was going on in their brain from the SPECT scan, they returned to the road of forward momentum. Their brains healed over time because they had the plan of action they needed.

Think about all this today. What is it that interferes with your unstoppability? What roadblock should be removed to go full speed forward, to let you begin to play that lovely musical melody of life that only you can do?

BIG CONCEPTS YOU LEARNED

Here's a list of the big concepts for this chapter:

- Girls with ADHD have more inattention than impulsivity.
- Less blood flow to the prefrontal cortex = more difficulty to focus
- Inattentiveness is not equal to stupidity!
- Boys with ADHD are more likely to be diagnosed.
- Parts of your brain function better than those without ADHD.
- Diagnosis needs someone competent to do it.
- The severity of ADHD is part of the diagnosis.
- SPECT scans may hold your solution.

2

MORE ABOUT YOUR DIAGNOSIS
AND CONSULTATION

You've already learned a lot about what happens during the consultation for the ADHD diagnosis. That's excellent forward momentum. You may have sensed some relief from worry about getting a diagnosis after learning the information on who does the diagnosis.

That first consultation should be expected to last a few hours. Much of this time may be spent filling out assessment forms. You can ask for all the forms to be filled out before the consultation to save time. Some doctors may not give you the forms until your first appointment or at the end of the appointment. They will spend time talking to you and your child during the consultation, collecting information from the questions they ask.

The clinician also will review information from your child's teachers and other adults. Statements made about your child from other professionals give insight into what's really going on.

For example, let's say that Sophia's teacher wrote a statement like this:

"Sophie is brilliant at times in class, and she amazes me with her insight into things we talk about in class. But most of the time, it looks like she has checked out. Her mind is somewhere else. Even when she's with other children, she does this, and it distances them from her."

Your doctor uses these types of statements for the diagnosis. This statement tells the doctor she could have moderate to severe ADHD.

Your clinician will also discuss these topics:

- What a typical day is like in your child's life. What's working and what's not?
- Medical history
- Family history – whether anyone else had similar issues
- Strengths and weaknesses – what your child focuses on (art, sports, computer work, singing, etc.)
- Education about ADHD – what the parent knows about it is brought up, and the clinician will discuss how symptoms are managed

WHAT'S THE DOCTOR'S GOAL DURING THIS APPOINTMENT?

This appointment aims to determine whether or not you have ADHD and rule out other conditions such as autism, learning disabilities, mood disorders, and auditory processing disorders.

If you are the one whom the appointment is about, it's best to bring another adult with you who spends a significant amount of time with you. This interview will not be so much about symptoms of adult ADHD but rather a hunt for any possible medical condition that may mimic ADHD.

This is where the additional assessment tests such as ADHD rating scales, IQ tests, and broad-spectrum scales that screen for psychiatric, emotional, and social conditions come into the picture. Tests on language development, vocabulary, memory recall, and motor skills, computer tests that ask a child to follow visual targets on the screen, and brain scans may be part of the data for the diagnosis.

WHY SOME DOCTORS WON'T DO COMPUTER TESTS OR BRAIN SCANS

There's something else you should know. The American Academy of Child and Adolescent Psychiatry, a professional organization that determines what psychiatrists should and shouldn't do in practice, recommends not to do computer tests and brain scans.

They believe there's not enough clinically useful information obtained from them, plus the amounts of radiation in a brain scan may be harmful. They say the brain scans are costly and usually not covered by insurance. Still, their images help parents and children understand why they are acting a certain way and may motivate them to get treatment.

The other point of view is from those who do these tests. Dr. Daniel Amen sees significant changes in the lives of those who have these scans and follows through on the treatment plans to boost the functions of the brain that need more activity while dampening the other hyperactive parts.

WHAT TYPES OF RATING SCALES CLINICIANS USE

The rating scales and assessments listed below tell you what doctors are looking for.

1. Behavior Assessment System for Children (BASC) – This assessment uncovers hyperactivity, aggression, learning or conduct issues, attention problems, depression, and anxiety. These symptoms are key to the diagnosis of ADHD.

2. Conners Scale for ADHD Assessment – This one is called the Conners Adult ADHD Rating Scale if it's given to an adult.

It tells your doctor how your symptoms impact life at home, relationships, school, and other areas. The questions cover hyperactivity, inattention, emotional problems, impulsiveness and compulsiveness, problems with math, eating, sleeping or keeping friends, temper tantrums, and fear of being separated from loved ones.

The rating scale for these ranges from 0 to 3, where 0 means it's never a problem and 3 means it happens very often. If you score less than 60, you don't have ADHD. If your score is > 60, you may have ADHD. If your score is > 70, you have more severe symptoms of ADHD.

It's also used to show how well you are improving later on.

3. Brown Attention-Deficit Disorder Symptom Assessment Scale (BADDS) for Adults – This is a 40-question assessment on memory, attention, and mood. These questions may be asked during an interview one-on-one with a clinician. This one is directly related to women with ADHD.

4. Vanderbilt Assessment Scale – While symptoms of ADHD are included on this one, the goal is to identify anyone with depression, anxiety, conduct disorder, and oppositional defiant disorder. These four must be deter-

mined to prevent a misdiagnosis and include a co-diagnosis if needed.

If the assessment is used for a child, questions are asked about sociability and how well the child is doing with schoolwork.

5. Child Behavior Checklist/Teacher Report Form (CBCL) – This assessment your teacher fills out about your behavior and social skills. It looks for physical complaints, aggression, and withdrawal. Teacher input plays a vital role in any ADHD diagnosis.

6. Tests of Variable Attention (TOVA) – This test discovers your ability to pay attention to tasks you don't like doing. This assessment is always used in conjunction with other reviews.

7. Adult ADHD Self-Report Scale (ASRS) – This test looks for ADHD symptoms in adults.

Health professionals will use these rating scales to help diagnose ADHD. And as mentioned before, qualified specialists in ADHD use them.

MEDICATION TREATMENTS FOR ADHD

Now this section won't make much sense to you if you haven't been prescribed a medication already. There's no need to memorize all the information here; just use it as a section to come back to later when you need it.

The goal for ADHD treatment by modern medicine is similar to treatments for other health disorders: to relieve symptoms and offer a higher quality of life. They are not a permanent cure.

Treatment is often medications and/or therapy. A qualified physician, usually a psychiatrist or pediatrician, always prescribes the treatment. Once prescribed, the primary care physician will monitor your ADHD condition.

The two primary types of medications are:

1. **Stimulants.** These may increase dopamine and norepinephrine or they may be amphetamines. Stimulants are usually fast-acting. Stimulants should not be mixed with antidepressants such as SSRIs, SNRIs, tricyclic antidepressants, and monoamine oxidase inhibitors.

2. **Nonstimulants.** Non-stimulant effects last up to 24 hours.

The medications may be taken daily or only on school days, depending on the prescription. They are not taken continually. Initially, children take low doses that increase over time. A medication break may be recommended during treatment to evaluate whether or not it should be continued.

Now that you know the big picture about medications, let's dive deeper and give you the five top medications and their brand names. This way you can identify them more easily:

1. Methylphenidate – Adhansia XR, Aptensio XR, Concerta, Cotempla XR-ODT, Jornay PM, Quilli-Chew ER, Quillivant XR, Relxxi, Ritalin LA, and generics
2. Lisdexamfetamine – Vyvanse
3. Dexamfetamine – Dexedrine, Dextrostat, Xelstrym
4. Atomoxetine – Strattera
5. Guanfacine – Intuniv XR

The stimulants are methylphenidate, lisdexamfetamine, and dexamfetamine.

Now let's find out what these drugs target, how they come (capsules, etc.), who they are usually prescribed to, and what are their side effects.

1. **Methylphenidate** – Targets brain areas that control behavior and attention. It's prescribed to anyone with ADHD over the age of 5.

There are three possible forms: 1) immediate-release tablets that are taken two to three times a day, 2) modified-release tablets taken in the morning (the dose is released throughout the day), or 3) a transdermal patch called Daytrana. (similar to Ritalin).

Side effects of methylphenidate include headaches, stomachaches, sleeping problems, loss of appetite, increased heart rate and blood pressure, and emotional symptoms such as depression, anxiety, irritability, or aggressiveness.

2. **Lisdexamfetamine** – Targets brain areas for attention, concentration, and behavior, especially impulsive behavior. For teens and children with ADHD older than 5 who have not benefitted from at least six weeks of treatment with methylphenidate. Adults may be offered this medication as the first choice of medication.

Lisdexamfetamine is taken once a day in capsule form. Side effects include headaches, dizziness, drowsiness, diarrhea, nausea and vomiting, aggression, and decreased appetite.

3. **Dexamfetamine** – Works like Lisdexamfetamine. Prescribed to anyone with ADHD over the age of 5. The dosage is in tablet form, taken twice to four times daily, or as a liquid. It's an amphetamine.

The side effects of this medication include headaches, dizziness, diarrhea, nausea and vomiting, decreased appetite, mood swings, and agitation/aggression.

4. **Atomoxetine** – This selective noradrenaline reuptake inhibitor (SNRI) medication increases noradrenaline levels in the brain. The drug improves concentration and impulsivity by passing messages between brain cells.

It's for those over the age of 5 who cannot use methylphenidate or Lisdexamfetamine and for any adults with ADHD. The capsules are taken once or twice daily.

Side effects include headaches, dizziness, stomachaches, nausea and vomiting, increased heart rate and blood pressure, yellowing skin or eye whites, and irritability. However, suicidal thoughts and liver damage may occur as well.

5. **Guanfacine** – Targets the brain to improve attention and lower blood pressure. Usually used to lower high blood pressure in adults. For teens and children older than 5 if methylphenidate or Lisdexamfetamine can't be used. It's NOT for adults with ADHD.

The medication is taken in tablet form once a day, either in the morning or evening. Side effects include headache, dry mouth, tiredness/fatigue, and abdominal pain.

THERAPIES FOR ADHD

Therapy can help anyone, not just those with ADHD. We all have perplexing things in our lives, situations we don't know how to navigate, and feelings we need help bringing to the surface to resolve. All these things can and will block our progress.

Talking to others, learning how to manage behavior and social skills, and parent training programs are available for those with ADHD and for their families. Therapies may also be effective in dealing with anxiety disorders.

Below is a list of some of these therapies:

1. **Cognitive behavioral therapy**

Often, a simple reframe of how you think about something that happened is enough to resolve the situation in your mind and soul. This talking therapy addresses how your child feels about something that happened, and challenges thought processes and behaviors. It may be an individual treatment or in a group.

2. **Psychoeducation**

This therapy is all about dealing with the diagnosis of ADHD and coping better daily with it.

3. **Behavior Therapy**

Parents, caregivers of a child with ADHD, and teachers benefit from this therapy by learning how to use rewards to change the child's behavior over time. The techniques taught present a way to identify specific behaviors to work toward and how to reward those behaviors.

Behavior therapy may include learning organizational skills and peer interventions focusing on behavior. Teachers learn how to plan and structure different activities for children and how to give children kudos for their progress.

There's a difference in how behavior therapy is used for children based on age. Behavior therapy is important for children younger than six and should be used before medication is given. When used this way, the whole family benefits because parents now have ways to help their children. It reduces some of the frustrations that parents have.

Children older than six usually benefit from medication along with behavior therapy.

4. Social Skills Training

Role-playing in social situations opens up the mind to options. This social skills training involves role-playing for your child, emphasizing how to behave. When children learn how their actions affect others, they change their behavior automatically.

5. Diet and Supplements

Some people notice a change in a behavior after consuming food. By keeping a food and behavior diary, patterns may emerge. After about a month, a clinical nutritionist, dietitian, or primary care physician qualified to analyze the data could be contacted. Ensure they have enough time to explore the data for the patterns.

Supplements may also be taken, but a complete nutritional workup needs to be done by a qualified professional to determine which ones would be best and for what length of time. Supplements should never be hit-or-miss or guesses.

TIPS YOU MAY ALREADY BE INCORPORATING

Below are nine different small tips that actually can bring big gains in how you handle your ADHD.

1. Upgrade to a healthy lifestyle.

This means nutritious food, regular exercise, and sound sleep. If any of these are out of balance, symptoms of ADHD will worsen.

2. Address planning help.

Learning how to plan is a skill that helps everyone. Do you need it? There are classes on it that are available.

3. Routines matter.

It's easy to think we are special and don't need routines, but when you start organizing your day according to routines, it really helps set expectations for the day.

4. Knowing your learning styles enhances academic progress.

You don't have to be a child to know your learning style. How you learn is unique to you during your entire life. When your environment matches your learning style, you work less on any project. Everyone needs adequate light and enough space to complete work, but some do better when music plays in the background. It is important to avoid high electromagnetic fields in your environment as they can disrupt your concentration.

5. Build your organization skills.

When you have a permanent place to put personal things such as keys, groceries, books, clothing, etc., they are easier to find later.

6. Instructions should be clear.

At work, don't proceed on a project when instructions are not clear. Ask all the questions initially and after about 30 minutes into the project.

REFLECTIONS

With this information, you are well set on knowing enough about the consultation and what happens after the diagnosis. Understanding this ahead of time keeps your forward momentum going. Since you'll know what to do next, you won't get tripped up if your doctor decides you need a few extra assessments or if your medication doesn't work well. You know about the options. You are unstoppable. Nothing is going to stop your progress.

BIG CONCEPTS YOU LEARNED

Here's a list of the big concepts for this chapter:

- The diagnosis comes from other people's statements about you, plus assessment results.
- Stimulants increase dopamine and norepinephrine. Non-stimulants may be prescribed.
- Expect side effects from medications.
- Therapies can give you new skills.

In the next chapter, one of the biggest stumbling blocks to women will be discussed. What might it be? Hint: It's something cyclical.

3

HOW HORMONES AFFECT WOMEN

Becky hits puberty, and her Adderal doesn't work anymore.

Emma's PMS worsens the week before menstruation, and heaven forbid a project is due at work that same week.

Mandy is utterly unfocused at work after ovulation. She experiences irritability, impulsivity, and forgetfulness that she can't seem to get a handle on.

Wendy was emotionally balanced and had learned effective strategies to manage her ADHD. They worked fine until she had a hysterectomy. That's when everything went awry with her emotions.

All these are examples of women with ADHD who are affected by hormonal changes.

So, how are hormones affected, and why would women with hormonal changes seem to be affected more than those who don't have ADHD?

WHAT DO WE KNOW SO FAR?

First, let's get into a bit of background on the problem. Women with ADHD are generally diagnosed between 36 and 38 if they are not diagnosed as a child. They may have been diagnosed with a mood disorder or anxiety disorder as a child. Mood disorders affect hormones and may be influenced by reproductive hormones.

However, getting treated for a mood disorder still does not address ADHD. As you learned before, there are physical changes in the brain that occur that may give someone with ADHD a disadvantage.

According to researchers, many doctors have been missing the impact of hormone fluctuations on ADHD. Since the brain is one of the targets for estrogen and progesterone to act upon, it impacts cognition, sleep, and mood. It makes sense that hormone fluctuations at different stages of a woman's life can profoundly influence their quality of life at different periods.

RELATIONSHIP OF HORMONES AND ADHD IN WOMEN

The relationship between hormones and ADHD goes hand in hand with estrogen and progesterone levels. Look for this during the different stages in a woman's life below. See if you can predict what times of a woman's life will have more ADHD symptoms than usual.

Women's hormones are ever-changing during their lives. During puberty, there are rising levels of estrogen and progesterone. Estrogen promotes the release of serotonin and dopamine, the two feel-good neurotransmitters.

Higher estrogen levels seem to increase the effectiveness of ADHD medications, while the opposite is true for progesterone. Progesterone slows your ability to process sensory stimuli. Thus, it can affect your ability to accurately feel what's happening in your emotions.

HOW PMS AND MENSTRUATION AFFECT WOMEN WITH ADHD

When periods start in a woman's life, there are monthly fluctuations in estrogen, progesterone, and testosterone. The first two weeks of a menstrual cycle are characterized by a slow and steady estrogen rise with lower levels of progesterone. This is why many women feel especially good during this time – including those with ADHD.

Then, during the luteal phase, which occurs during the last two weeks of the cycle, progesterone levels are higher, and estrogen is low. These changes may end up reducing the effectiveness of stimulant medications. They may also affect women's ADHD symptoms more severely if they already have severe PMS and ADHD.

These last two weeks are when it's tougher to get things done. Other symptoms that may show up include depression (from the lower feel-good neurotransmitters), mood swings (the hippocampus is involved, too), anxiety, confusion, sleep problems, fatigue, and irritability).

During pregnancy, levels of estrogen are higher. They seem to prevent ADHD symptoms from getting worse. However, the hormone fluctuations in the first trimester can be a little rough on a woman with ADHD regarding moods and family functioning, according to one small study.

On the other hand, some women with ADHD say they never felt better than during their pregnancy. The higher estrogen levels keep them happy and productive.

POSTPARTUM CHANGES

But after giving birth, there's a rapid fall of estrogen, and symptoms may worsen temporarily while hormones are readjusting. The drop in estrogen can worsen ADHD symptoms and depression. Plus, all the effects of stress and lack of sleep have a way of bringing out ADHD symptoms once again.

In one Journal of Psychiatric Research report in 2021, psychologists studied 209 women with ADHD between 18 and 71. They found that the women had a higher prevalence of premenstrual dysphoric disorder (PMDD) and episodes of postpartum depression symptoms after their first childbirth compared to the general population. PMDD is a more severe form of PMS.

Those who had the PMDD symptoms did not take oral contraceptives. And if they were taking antidepressants, they had more PMDD symptoms. They also suffered more menopausal symptoms. This was the first study in women with ADHD that suggests that female ADHD patients suffer more.

CHANGES IN THE OLDER YEARS

During perimenopause, a woman's reproductive hormone levels again start falling. The fluctuating levels may worsen ADHD symptoms. That's when difficulty focusing, memory issues, and moodiness also appear.

By menopause, the estrogen has dropped by about 60%. The estrogen levels have stabilized, so worsening ADHD symptoms may require additional ADHD medication or hormone replacement.

Hormones definitely impact women, whether or not they have ADHD. Studies are now showing that sex hormones help regulate how well brain cells communicate with each other. They can also affect executive function, one of the brain's most critical areas in those with ADHD. Executive functions allow us to plan, make decisions, remember information, think flexibly, strategize our future, and control our actions.

ADHD symptoms may worsen during menopause because of the lack of sex hormones. Ovarian hormones exert control over the brain synapses. When hormone replacement is given, the number of synapses increases in density. Thus, hormone replacement seems essential for its effects on brain structure, mood, and cognitive functioning in domains such as working memory and executive control.

EXPLAINING INDIVIDUAL ADHD CASES

We started out this chapter with a few cases. You could probably explain to yourself what happened in each of them. For clarity's sake, each will be described here.

1. Becky's Adderal doesn't work after she hits puberty.

Becky's hormone levels changed, and along with them, her metabolism ramped itself up. That means that any medications she was on would break down in the body faster. They wouldn't be as effective as before. But more important than this, some doctors report that ADHD medications are ineffective at puberty. That's when a change of medication may be needed.

2. Emma's PMS worsens the week before menstruation, and heaven forbid a project is due at work that same week.

PMS is a situation where the hormones are out of balance, so Emma is already out of balance before the normal hormonal fluctuations occur during the month. Her PMS worsens before menstruation. Menstruation is when progesterone levels are high, and estrogen levels are low.

3. Mandy is completely unfocused at work after ovulation. She experiences irritability, impulsivity, and forgetfulness that she can't seem to get a handle on.

Mandy is affected because of the low estrogen and high progesterone levels.

4. Wendy was emotionally balanced and had learned effective strategies to manage her ADHD. They worked fine until she had a hysterectomy. That's when everything went awry with her emotions.

Wendy's sudden low levels of estrogen caused her ADHD levels to worsen.

NOT DISCUSSED MUCH BY MODERN MEDICINE

One of the things you will rarely read about on the internet is the underlying causes of hormone disruptions. You have to ask yourself why some women will have PMS so severe that it's disabling while others don't notice any symptoms during their entire menstrual cycle. Could it be possible that there are differences in their nutritional status?

Yes, say researchers ... although modern medicine often prefers to look the other way and not address nutritional causes.

Why are we always rushing to conclude that there's a physiological but not nutritional deficiency? Why do medical people imply that the normal hormone cycling in the menstrual cycle hormones prove there is an imbalance? What if the nutritional issues were truly the cause?

Specific vitamins and minerals are required to synthesize hormones in the body. Without them, the job can't be done correctly. The following nutrients are used in the body for hormonal balance: Vitamin C and D, calcium, magnesium, B vitamins, boron, and omega-3 fish oils.

Vitamin C – Regulates cortisol and adrenaline, helps restore fertility, reduces gestational diabetes during pregnancy, restores the function of the left ventricle in postmenopausal women with low estrogen levels, reduces stress and anxiety.

Vitamin D – One of the master controllers of estrogen and progesterone activity, regulates insulin and blood sugar levels, helps manage thyroid diseases.

B vitamins – All steroid hormones, such as estrogen and progesterone, will be produced only when there's enough vitamin B5 (pantothenic acid). This B vitamin is also essential during the production of neurotransmitters.

Calcium – Estrogen receptors stimulate intracellular calcium release and progesterone synthesis in nerve cells in the hypothalamus. The calcium release is important for activating muscle contraction.

Magnesium – Mineral critical for the production of estrogen, progesterone, and testosterone, helps in the production of thyroid hormone and helps control insulin production.

Boron – Increases the concentration of estrogen and testosterone in the plasma.

Omega 3 fish oils – Decreases the vitamin D levels and increases the estrogen levels.

With this information quite clear, it makes me wonder why doctors aren't investigating the role of nutrient status in those who have hormonal imbalances, ADHD patients, and regular patients. Not having enough of the proper nutrients for hormonal balance can put a big stop to many things you are doing. And hormone balance is rough on the psyche.

What Studies Show

There was one excellent medical report about deficiencies that was written by some dietetic professionals from a Poland medical university. They studied pregnant women and were concerned about their children getting ADHD. You may not be pregnant now, but their medical report focused on how diet could be a big link to ADHD can shed light on the diet of anyone with ADHD.

Here's what they say in their own words:

"The diet of pregnant and lactating women and children may impact the development and deepening of the hyperkinetic syndrome. There is much evidence to indicate that it is linked to nutritional factors."

"Chronic deficiencies of certain minerals such as zinc, iron, magnesium, and iodine and insufficient dietary intake of long-chain polyunsaturated fatty acids may significantly impact the development and deepening of the symptoms of ADHD in children."

"Polyunsaturated omega-3 fatty acids, mainly DHA, which are necessary for proper brain development and function, play a crucial role in the diet of pregnant and lactating women and children. Their chronic deficiency may contribute to increased risk of ADHD in children... It was found that eating foods with a low glycemic index helps to reduce symptoms in some hyperactive children..."

Many online resources act as if they are defeated about having ADHD, especially ones written for parents, and consider hormonal imbalances as a way of life. For example, they'll say it's essential to identify your daughter's strengths and emphasize them during the worst times of her cycle. They want you to work around the imbalances, not solve them. But why not just look for the real cause of these hormonal imbalances. Remember that there's an underlying reason(s) why some women never get them and others do. Why agree with it?

Sure, there are coping mechanisms until you find the underlying cause. Symptoms may indeed worsen at certain times of the month. If you expect them to happen, you can complete schoolwork before they hit. You don't have to wait until the last minute to finish a big paper when you know your period is coming – along with symptoms.

Be bold and go a little farther to explore this nutrition avenue. If you want to be unstoppable, new areas must be considered.

BIG CONCEPTS IN THIS CHAPTER

Here's a list of the big concepts for this chapter:

- Women with ADHD are mostly diagnosed between the ages of 36 and 38.
- Co-existing mood disorders are possible.

- Hormone fluctuations matter and may worsen ADHD symptoms.
- Something as simple as diet and deficiencies could explain a lot.

In the next chapter, we'll do a deeper dive into some of the causes of ADHD as well as symptoms of ADHD.

4

NAVIGATING FURTHER: THE CAUSES, SIGNS, AND SYMPTOMS

> "I am not absentminded. It is the presence of mind that makes me unaware of everything else."
>
> — G.K. CHESTERTON

This quotation is pertinent to this chapter and the next chapter. Here in this chapter, time blindness is brought up. It's an example of how the brain of someone with ADHD can make them unaware of everything else. This can be either an advantage or disadvantage, depending on what type of activity the person is absorbed in.

In this chapter, you'll learn about procrastination, time blindness, and other symptoms that affect those with ADHD. But first, we'll do a deep dive into the causes of

ADHD and the differences in symptoms in adults vs. children.

CAUSES OF ADHD.

In this following text, do a little imaginative thinking. Think of society searching for the causes of ADHD and what it might look like if you were observing it from a bird's eye view.

Who started the whole search for the causes of ADHD? It may have been the mother or father of a child with ADHD. In ancient times, ancient thinkers, much like children asking why the sky is blue, pondered over humors and imbalances that might stir the spirit. Back then, these things caused disease, and everything was thought to be controlled by spirits.

Cause #1: Anatomical Causes

Then, as time flowed forward, more voices joined the chorus. "ADHD is caused by the anatomical structures of the brain," a few researchers said, confirming that some parts of the brain are smaller in kids. "Kids with ADHD can't be smart because of this," they may have said.

And that sparked a big controversy, as you could imagine. Parents with ADHD children were on one side of the room, with parents of children smart enough to join MENSA on the other side. Parents with ADHD brought big signs saying things like, "My ADHD daughter is brilliant. Wait 20 years and see."

In contrast, the snooty MENSA parents debated them vehemently. That's when the researchers stepped in and said the science was precise. The parts of the brain that were smaller in ADHD children take longer to develop. Their IQ will catch up! They silenced the MENSA children's parents, who thought their kids were better than ADHD kids.

The different parts of the brain that are associated with learning and memory include:

- Caudate nucleus – for decision-making and behaviors with purpose
- Cerebral cortex – for self-management. This part of the brain may take longer to mature in ADHD children. The ADHD brain simply needs more time to be organized more efficiently.
- Putamen – for learning, memory, and regulating movement
- Hippocampus – for working memory and long-term memory
- Amygdala – plays an essential role in emotional control and prioritizing action
- Nucleus accumbens – for mood, motivation, and experiencing pleasure

Cause #2: It's in the Genes

Geneticists became more well known in their profession and stepped into the dialogue. Reports came forward that ADHD frequently runs in families. Every child has a 25% to 50% chance that one of their parents has ADHD, plus there's a 30% likelihood that another family member has ADHD, too. Researchers started testing parents and their children together. They found that a lot more people had ADHD than what was ever expected. What happened to the parents could definitely occur in their children.

Cause #3: Brain Trauma

Other researchers didn't care about genetics and put their efforts into more likely causes of ADHD, such as head injuries. A head injury is a traumatic brain injury (TBI), and many of the symptoms of ADHD are similarly seen in those with head injuries. As it's pretty easy for young children to fall while learning how to walk, run, and bike, many parents felt like head injuries were the cause of ADHD for their children. A TBI was considered a cause of ADHD.

Cause #4: They Aren't Good Moms

Then came the researchers that may have seemed to some to have a vendetta against women. These scientists were convinced that ADHD was caused in the womb. Their research found that if the mom was drinking alcohol or smoking, there was a greater risk of developing ADHD. This was about the same time that moms were also blamed for their children getting diabetes decades after carrying those babies in the womb.

Cause #5: It's the Premies

Then, another similar group extended their search for causes of ADHD but dropped the blame against women. They found that prematurity increases the risk of developing ADHD – and often, a woman has nothing to do with whether or not her baby is born prematurely.

Cause #6: It's the Heavy Metal Lead in the Environment

Similarly, scientists found that when there's lead in the environment, it affects the brain and may lead to ADHD.

These are the six leading causes of ADHD.

WHAT DOESN'T CAUSE ADHD

Researchers who have looked at other possible causes have ruled out the following things:

- A diet of too much sugar. No particular food or meal plan has been proven to cause ADHD.
- Watching too much TV or playing video games

- Stress
- Poverty
- Bad parenting styles

Although all of the above certainly will influence a child with ADHD, they are not causes.

SIGNS AND SYMPTOMS OF ADULT ADHD

There's a myth about ADHD that applies to the category of symptoms. It's helpful to know about it. That myth is that everyone has ADHD symptoms and, therefore, has ADHD to a degree.

Anyone can indeed have similar symptoms of ADHD. Who hasn't felt inattentive at a boring presentation or impulsive when a pet does the same boo-boo one more time? However, there is a difference, and it has to do with the frequency of symptoms and severity and how they affect someone's quality of life. Those with chronic impairments that affect their lives more deeply are the ones who get diagnosed with ADHD.

Regarding how long adults keep having their ADHD symptoms, not all of them continue to have ADHD symptoms as they age. The remaining symptoms may include restlessness, difficulty paying attention, and impulsiveness. Adults with ADHD tend to miss deadlines and forget appointments, all based on an inability to focus and prioritize. If they have issues controlling impulses, then tasks such as driving or waiting in line, as examples, are still tricky. Friends and family members may still notice mood swings and anger outbursts.

In an earlier chapter, we listed the symptoms required for diagnosing ADHD according to the DSM-5. In the rest of this chapter, you'll find more specific lists of symptoms of ADHD for adults, children, teens, and girls/women.

SIGNS AND SYMPTOMS OF ADHD IN ADULTS

ADHD in adulthood affects various aspects of a person's life. While it often manifests differently compared to children, it is characterized by challenges in attention, focus, and impulsivity. Adults with ADHD often face unique struggles in their personal and professional lives.

Recognizing the signs and symptoms of ADHD in adults is vital for seeking appropriate diagnosis and support.

Here's the list:

- Impulsiveness
- Disorganization
- Difficulty prioritizing
- Poor time management skills
- Problems focusing on a task
- Hot temper
- Trouble coping with stress
- Low tolerance for frustration

- Frequent mood swings
- Trouble multitasking
- Poor planning
- Problems following through and completing tasks
- Excessive activity or restlessness
- Frequent accidents or injuries
- Substance misuse issues, especially with alcohol
- Difficulties at college, trouble passing classes

SIGNS AND SYMPTOMS OF ADHD IN CHILDREN

While kids are naturally full of energy and can be impulsive, children with ADHD may exhibit more persistent and challenging behaviors that can impact their ability to focus, learn, and interact with others. Recognizing the signs and symptoms of ADHD in children is crucial for parents, teachers, and caregivers to provide the necessary support and guidance for these young individuals.

Here is the list of their symptoms:

- Easily distracted and difficulty focusing on activities
- Short attention span for homework or even while playing
- Trouble sitting still, fidgety
- Feels like they must move constantly
- Loud or disruptive while engaging in activities
- Interrupts people

- Excess talking

SIGNS AND SYMPTOMS OF ADHD IN TEENS

While it's normal for teenagers to exhibit some degree of impulsivity and inattention during adolescence, ADHD presents a distinct set of symptoms. These often interfere with daily life. Recognizing these signs is essential in providing the necessary support and intervention to help teenagers thrive.

Here's a list of the symptoms you can expect to see in teens:

- Difficulty focusing on work or schoolwork
- Trouble finishing chores or schoolwork
- Organizing tasks and managing time is a big issue
- Family and social relationships are difficult
- ADHD symptoms cause problems with parents at home
- Forgets things and lose things
- Avoids mentally challenging tasks
- Makes lots of mistakes while doing work
- Frustration keeps increasing
- Emotionally fragile

SIGNS AND SYMPTOMS OF ADHD IN WOMEN AND GIRLS

Although women primarily experience symptoms in the inattentive category, they often experience hyperactive-impulsive symptoms as well. These in the latter arena may not be as severe as males with ADHD, but they still may exist.

Inattention symptoms include the following:

- Easily distracted
- Forgetful
- Difficulty listening to people
- Difficulty attending to details
- Attention span is short
- For their age, poor organizational skills and poor study skills

Impulsivity symptoms include the following:

- Can't have a conversation without interrupting others
- Can't wait for their turn in school or socially
- Blurts out answers in class
- Risk-taker, not thinking before acting

Hyperactivity symptoms include the following:

- Difficulty staying in their seat when they should
- Runs or climbs just for the sake of constant motion
- Excessive talking
- Frequently loses and/or forgets things
- Can't stay on task, shifts to other things without finishing any of them
- Difficulty engaging in activities that require quiet

Other symptoms of ADHD in girls and women include:

- Greater likelihood of bullying or other severe social problems
- Severe challenges in academics and self-esteem
- Increased risk of STDs
- Increased risk of pregnancy
- Severe difficulties with mood changes and regulation of emotions
- Increased compensational behaviors that are used at home, school, or work
- Symptoms worsened with hormonal changes during menstrual cycles, pregnancy, or menopause

Additional symptoms that may be included in the category of trouble concentrating include:

- Being bombarded with many thoughts simultaneously, making it challenging to follow only one of them
- Difficulty reading
- "Zoning out" of a conversation or frequent daydreaming
- Having a difficult time following directions
- Getting quickly bored and needing new stimulating experiences

MASKING

Some symptoms are not generally included in the criteria for an ADHD diagnosis. Still, they appear quite often in those with ADHD. Masking is one of them.

What is Masking?

When someone has ADHD, they develop coping skills to try to adapt to their weaknesses. ADHD masking is a way to relieve insecure feelings by trying to act normal – at the expense of one's mental health. It's a way to hide ADHD in public settings, suppress symptoms, and deny the effects felt by ADHD. It's a way that is believed to show others everything is under control, a form of faking life.

The term was coined by Russell Barkley in 2010, and it is estimated that about one-third of all neurodiverse people do masking. ADHD can begin pre-adolescence when children learn to fit in society and determine one's best daily routine.

However, ADHD masking may not manifest in a person until certain situations show up, such as when a new job is started. Entering college is another time it may show up, as they have to fit into society differently. In these unique situations, there's a risk or fear the person feels – that they will miss out on something, so they resort to masking.

Let's take a look at the ADHD symptoms with their corresponding masking behaviors in the table below:

ADHD Symptom	Masked Behavior (Example – Someone with ADHD…)
Not listening to others	Guesses about what the conversation is about or listens carefully and focuses hard so nothing is missed in the conversation
Forgetfulness	Tries to get the answer about what they forgot from another person in the conversation or write everything down in notes
Emotionalism	Bottles up their emotions and then feels sick or depressed
Careless mistakes	Starts blaming others for his careless mistakes
Losing items	Blames kids, spouse, or dog for taking keys and other items or obsessively checks their belongings
Unable to engage in leisure activities, relax, or unwind	Says his motivation to do things has to be attended to
Fidgetiness	Claims their clothes are making them itch, or their chair is very uncomfortable, or keeps his arms folded in front of himself to avoid fidgeting
Excessively talking and interrupting others	Tries to appear as a happy, energetic, and engaged person
Late for appointments	Cancels appointments if it's obvious they will be late for that appointment
Disorganized	Spends exceptional amounts of time trying to get organized for a project
Talking too much	Sends texts to people after conversations saying they are sorry for talking so much

CONSEQUENCES OF MASKING

Masking is pretending to be someone else and not being transparent. There's a lot of negative thinking involved in masking. The person conceals their identity, and there's a lack of authenticity. When someone isn't true to themselves, there will always be a disconnect between who they really are and who they believe they should be. This can affect how they feel about their future goals.

Other consequences include:

- Extreme fatigue just from the amount of energy it takes to put up a false front
- Possible perfectionistic tendencies so that a mistake won't ever be made
- Delayed diagnosis of ADHD, limiting access to treatment
- Loss of sense of self
- Having a sense of shame
- Increased stress and burnout
- Not acknowledging that help is needed and thus not sought
- Others don't believe they are struggling emotionally
- Higher risk for substance abuse problems
- Over time, there's an inability to distinguish what is real and what is an act

Masking can be replaced by a better solution: focusing on one's strengths instead of one's weaknesses and developing emotional regulation skills through counseling or classes. When training starts, it's good to know that part of the process requires analyzing how your ADHD symptoms affect you and listing the scenarios that trigger you to engage in masking. From there, the true healing begins.

TIME BLINDNESS

Time blindness is another of the symptoms that shows up in those with ADHD, but it may also show up in others without ADHD. Thus, it's not on the criteria list for diagnosis.

WHAT IS TIME BLINDNESS?

Time blindness is a term that was coined in 2001 about the inability to sense the passing of time correctly. It's not intentional but more like a sensory issue arising from the nervous system. It happens to those who have ADHD.

When you perceive time, your brain uses your heart rate. It adds the environment's brightness and temperature changes to determine how much time passes. Researchers call this concept the scalar expectancy theory (SET).

Time blindness shows up in any of these ways:

- "Losing track of time"
- Feeling like time is "slipping away"
- Missing deadlines or showing up late for appointments
- Gauging incorrectly how long a task will take or how much time is left before an event
- Feeling like making a schedule is a lost cause because you can't stick to it
- Slow reaction times
- Don't feel a deadline inching closer
- Feeling like you are stuck in the present (especially for those who are impulsive)
- When presented with two activities, you aren't sure which will take the longest.
- Difficulty regulating how fast or slow you do things
- Difficulty estimating when events happened, even ones such as when you ate breakfast or your last vacation
- Burning food on the stove because you thought it would cook for 10 minutes, but it's been an hour
- Thinking you are capable of doing much more in one day than anyone could do

Someone with ADHD may do well on tasks that get them emotionally charged. Still, in situations where they are emotionally neutral, they can't seem to get timing correct, according to one study. This may occur because strong emotional stimuli cause heart rate changes, disrupting the internal clock.

Researchers have also found that time blindness in those with ADHD may be due to dopamine deficiencies. When subjects took prescription stimulants and were offered monetary rewards, they improved their time perception. Stimulants increase dopamine levels.

Time blindness has been proposed as a new symptom to add to the symptom list for a possible diagnosis of ADHD. It's relevant to the life of someone with ADHD.

CONSEQUENCES OF TIME BLINDNESS

There are consequences of time blindness. Others begin believing your character is flawed because you aren't on time. They may also see you as someone who overestimates their abilities or you are slow, incompetent, and irresponsible. You may feel like life is passing you by.

Low self-esteem and poor relationships with others and self are also expected consequences. Experiencing incidents of time blindness also puts those with ADHD at a five times higher risk for deliberate self-harm.

COPING WITH TIME BLINDNESS

ADHD medications are beneficial in those with time blindness.

Some additional ways to cope with time blindness include:

- Get a coach to help you improve executive function skills.
- Utilize time-tracking apps that show how long it takes you to do specific tasks
- Start doing things that increase dopamine production in the body, such as getting sunlight, exercising, and taking your B vitamins (vitamin B6 raises dopamine levels.).
- Decide how long you will participate in an activity at the start of an activity.
- Double how long an activity will take to get the timing correct.
- Listen to music. Background music may give your brain another external cue to track time and help you get back on track.

REFLECTIONS

The six causes of ADHD can give us insight into what are the root causes of one's initial onset of ADHD. However, getting locked in on the causes doesn't do anything to help us move forward.

Symptoms vary slightly for those who are adults versus children and teens.

Symptoms such as masking and time blindness are common in those with ADHD but there are strategies that can be used to deal with them successfully. An example of masking one's emotions is that of stuffing one's feelings and not letting others see how one truly feels. Once you start to master these weaknesses of masking and time blindness, you make progress towards being the unstoppable person you were meant to be.

BIG CONCEPTS IN THIS CHAPTER

Here's a list of the big concepts for this chapter:

- ADHD Causes: It's anatomical. It's in the genes. Brain trauma. Blame it on mom. It's the premies. It's heavy metals.
- What doesn't cause ADHD: sugar, stress, poverty, bad parenting, too much TV
- That myth is that everyone has ADHD symptoms and, therefore, has ADHD to a degree.
- Signs and symptoms are specific for age and for women.
- Masking = not authentic; people won't know who you are

- Masking can be replaced by focusing on one's strengths instead of one's weaknesses and developing emotional regulation skills through counseling or classes.
- Time blindness = stuck in a time warp by yourself; others have to get you out
- Time blindness responds to getting more sunlight and taking your B vitamins.

In the next chapter, we'll learn some additional symptoms that aren't necessarily included in the diagnostic criteria for ADHD plus information about the ADHD Tax.

5

PROCRASTINATION, THE ADHD TAX, AND HYPERFOCUS

"I am not absentminded. It is the presence of mind that makes me unaware of everything else."

— G.K. CHESTERTON

The hyperfocus that a child or adult with ADHD puts them into a state of mind that keeps them oblivious to everything else going on around them. This can be to their advantage or disadvantage, depending on the type of results achieved with the activity and what is being neglected.

In this chapter, you'll learn about procrastination, the ADHD tax, and hyperfocus.

PROCRASTINATION

Although everyone procrastinates to an extent, you can count on those with ADHD – especially those who have not had the chance to work on this bad habit – to have it.

WHAT IS PROCRASTINATION?

Procrastination is avoiding a task or decision that must be completed by a specific deadline.

Although everyone tends to put off some tasks, those with ADHD never get procrastinated tasks done.

RELATIONSHIP BETWEEN ADHD AND PROCRASTINATION

Researchers don't believe there's a direct relationship between ADHD and procrastination. However, they do agree that there are specific ADHD characteristics that make it most likely for those with ADHD to procrastinate.

Although one study in 2014 found that inattention in those with ADHD was the only quality correlated with postponing tasks, other symptoms may be related. Healthcare professionals do not include procrastination in the DSM-5 criteria for diagnosing ADHD.

Other experts believe that those with ADHD are more likely to procrastinate because of these symptoms:

- forgetfulness
- disorganization
- susceptible to distractions
- time management problems
- hyperactivity/impulsivity
- prioritization issues
- inattention
- impaired sense of time
- tendency to avoid tasks that require a lot of mental work
- difficulty in staying on task and staying motivated
- fear of failure

In fact, the more symptoms that someone has for ADHD, and the more severe that they are, the more likely they are likely to procrastinate.

Another aspect of procrastination is the combination of perfectionism and procrastination. Perfectionism procrastination is when someone does not complete a task because they believe it cannot be done perfectly.

Other Types of Procrastination

There are a few other types of procrastination that those with ADHD could experience:

1. Academic procrastination

This type of procrastination is related to completing tasks related to coursework. It could include procrastinating studying or even deciding not to take a test because the test score result would not reflect the perfectionism about the topic they have about themselves in their mind. Writing research papers or essays are the academic tasks that are the most likely to be procrastinated. Dyslexia or any other learning disabilities may also be a part of academic procrastination.

2. Everyday procrastination

This type of procrastination is related to doing the dishes, cleaning the car or garage, not taking the garbage out until the garbage truck is on its way down the street, and not doing laundry until it piles up to an awful pile.

3. Decisional procrastination

This type of delay in taking action is related to making different decisions. Some of them may include making all the phone calls to car insurance companies but not making the final decision, not making a decision related to a child or a spouse, and not making a decision related to a vacation until too late.

People with ADHD may procrastinate because of anxiety or depression as well. This is why it's so important to ensure that the assessment process for diagnosing ADHD includes ruling out or diagnosing a co-existing mental disorder.

CONSEQUENCES OF CHRONIC PROCRASTINATION

Below are five of the most common consequences of chronic procrastination.

1. When bills aren't paid on time, it can cause financial stress in the home.

2. Extra stress at home or work when tasks are not completed until the last minute.

3. Relationship problems when you put off others, making them feel like you don't value them

4. Frustration, shame, guilt, and low self-esteem

5. Depression and anxiety from internalizing negative feelings

SOME SOLUTIONS FOR PROCRASTINATION

Procrastination isn't a permanent trait. It can be changed.

Below are some strategies that help you transform from being a procrastinator to a doer.

1. ADHD medication may help a lot!

2. Reduce big projects into smaller ones and feel victory after each minor job completion.

3. Give yourself a reward for finishing the project.

4. Go for complete immersion into the task with few distractions.

5. Consider a type of treatment called acceptance and commitment therapy (ACT). This treatment may help you decide why you procrastinate.

6. Work on better organizational skills. Part of the organization may include scheduling work according to times when you are more productive, creating routines, improving your work environment, and more.

7. Set reminders for yourself.

8. Get enough rest. When you don't get enough sleep, it isn't easy to be at your top level of productivity.

9. Forgive yourself for times you procrastinated in the past. Develop some self-compassion.

ADHD TAX

"I missed my deadlines for student loan payments, and now an extra $50,000 of attorney's fees have been added to the bill."

"Today, I decided to clean the fridge and threw out a garbage bag full of things I didn't eat. Then I got the grocery store receipts out; the total was $65.78."

"My assistant came over and had been helping me with my overdue taxes. Then she told me how bad it was that I couldn't get my taxes in on time, and who did I think I was to think it was okay to be late?"

"I was getting ready to sell my car when the potential buyer asked for the records of oil changes. I did the first oil change but never did it after that. Also, I never took the car in for the recalls."

"I have a stack of unopened bills. Sometimes I wake up, and there's no electricity or phone, and I always trace it back to not opening those bills."

All these are examples of the ADHD Tax.

WHAT IS THE ADHD TAX?

The ADHD tax is not a tax from the government. It's the tax you pay for not completing things on time due to procrastination and other ADHD symptoms. It's money you lost from yourself because of your ADHD symptoms. Some define it as the gap between intention and actions or the price you pay for costly mistakes due to your symptoms. It's expensive to have ADHD!

The official definition is the extra costs those with diagnosable inattention, hyperactivity, impulsivity, and/or executive function challenges incur due to inattentive, hyperactive, impulsive, and/or struggling with executive function.

The ADHD tax is usually about financial costs. An estimated cost of ADHD for children and adults is anywhere from $800 to $20,000. The numbers could be so high due to juvenile justice costs, healthcare costs, educational costs, and loss of wages.

Some examples of specific costs are listed below:

- late fees
- missed flights costs
- higher interest rates
- lost checks
- library books or other things not returned on time
- courses that we never finished
- services we didn't use
- charges for missed doctor or dentist appointments
- food that perished in the refrigerator
- not returning clothes that didn't fit on time

- rush shipping costs
- spending too much on presents
- credit profile damage
- delaying job education that could lead to promotion

CONSEQUENCES OF ADHD TAX

One study found that these costs add up over the years. They contribute to becoming financially independent much later in life than those who don't have ADHD. In fact, one estimate is that those with ADHD make $1 million less in their lifetime than those without ADHD.

The truth is that hidden costs are difficult to calculate. How can you put a price on mental health, personal freedom (instead of incarceration), and physical well-being? And supposedly, those with ADHD die 13 years earlier than those who don't have ADHD. That's because if you're distracted, you're more prone to accidents both on the road and on the job. Other things contributing to that loss of lifespan include the consequences of lack of sleep, poor diet, lack of exercise, neglect of dental care and health care, use of alcohol and drugs, and more.

The ADHD tax can also take a toll on and cost you:

- time
- relationships – depending financially on family members
- health – For example, you don't have any extra cash for wellness services.

When you sit down and calculate your ADHD tax, it's common to experience guilt and shame, poor self-esteem, and strained relationships that lead to broken trust. But things like damaged credit can follow you for the next 10 years. However, you can reduce these costs when you gain more control over your ADHD symptoms.

SOME SOLUTIONS FOR YOU TO HANDLE THE ADHD TAX

There are many solutions for the ADHD Tax. There's hope!

Check out some of these solutions:

1. Join a support group, such as one hosted by ADDA and CHADD, specifically for dealing with this.
2. Take a class from RenaFi.com, a financial company that caters to those with ADHD.
3. Tackle the different areas that you are paying the ADHD tax, one by one. Develop strategies for it

and then progress forward to the next one.

4. Get an accountability partner.
5. Counsel yourself on purchases with questions such as "If I don't do this now, what are the consequences?" and "If I do this now, what opportunities will manifest for me?"
6. Confront difficult situations that you really don't want to address. This helps you step out of paralysis.
7. Check your medication with your doctor. Is it helping you beat procrastination and the ADHD tax? If not, maybe the dosage should be increased.
8. Quarterly, re-evaluate all your online subscriptions. Do you really need them?
9. Reconsider any impulse spending.
10. Learn meal planning. Limit take-out dinners and eating out because you run out of time to do other things.

"IN THE ZONE" AND HYPERFOCUS

A successful writer will often tell you they need significant periods of time to write. That's because those times are periods of intense concentration. During those times, they may write for hours because they are engrossed in what they are doing.

There's a difference between being in the zone and hyperfocus. You'll learn more in-depth about the zone in the next chapter.

WHAT IS HYPERFOCUS?

Hyperfocus is when you are exceptionally focused on something for a very long period and lose track of everything else going on around you. Hyperfocus happens on things you enjoy doing. It's a part of being human to get interested in something and lose track of time. Think of new lovers!

Hyperfocus is seen in those with ADHD, but it's not an official symptom registered in the DSM-5 for diagnosis. It's a controversial symptom, primarily because you won't find many studies on it. But it's also seen in other non-ADHD people.

You could say that the difference between those with ADHD and those without ADHD in terms of hyperfocus is that those with ADHD become oblivious to everything else happening around them. They lose track of real-time and what they should have done (work or home chores). They need help switching their attention to something else, such as pressing responsibilities.

Hyperfocus is common in those with traumatic brain injury, schizophrenia, and autism.

How you feel when you are in hyperfocus depends on what you are doing. It may feel like you have disconnected from yourself and your environment. It might give you euphoric feelings. And you may have pinpointed laser focus.

Many people agree that hyperfocus is a key to their success. But it does alienate you from others – family members and friends who sometimes depend on your presence. Hyperfocus can make you late for appointments because you might lose track of time. So hyperfocus can have a good and bad side to it. College students with ADHD often intentionally go into a state of hyperfocus to get their homework done. They do it effortlessly.

In these electronic times, getting super absorbed in video games, social media, computer work you love, and watching television is easy. What researchers have found is that there are frontal lobe changes that occur in the brain that make hyperfocus more likely to happen. Hyperfocus is also believed to arise from abnormally low levels of dopamine. Dopamine is active in the frontal lobes.

Let's dive a little deeper.

There are two types of attention – automatic and directed. When attention is automatic, then you don't control it. Hyperfocus is a form of automatic attention that happens when you are absorbed in something that interests you. It could be a phone conversation, a craft, a television show, or anything else.

Directed attention requires your energy. For example, doing the dishes or paying attention to a boring class. To do these types of actions, you use directed attention to turn off automatic attention. Directed attention is associated with the executive functions of the brain. Because the process of directed attention requires energy, that's why you feel too wiped out to do anything after doing these activities.

In those with ADHD, the overall problem is that you can't seem to control your attention, not that you lack the ability to have attention. Thus, your attention wants to go in one direction, but you want it to go somewhere else. Thus, hyperfocus results from a lack of control.

Curbing your hyperfocus is knowing what kind of things automatically grab your attention and limiting them at certain times of the day or limiting how long you are engrossed.

For example, you wouldn't want to start engaging in a hyperfocus activity before bedtime or when you have an appointment that you cannot miss.

Another way to deal with hyperfocus is to take regular breaks during a hyperfocus activity. This works because the breaks reset your brain. You can also change screen time settings on your phone to limit your activities.

One additional technique is to give yourself "When-Then" contingency breaks. For example, only when you finish your homework can you have lunch. The secret to managing hyperfocus is to create structure around activities that lend themselves to getting into the zone.

THE PROS AND CONS OF HYPERFOCUS

There aren't any ADHD medications that will stop hyperfocus. You can't manage it internally. It would help if you had something from the real world to get you out of your head. So it distracts you from important tasks you have to do. And if it's used to play video games or other unproductive things, it's a waste of time. It interferes with relationships, productivity, and academic work.

However, many writers, artists, and scientists positively use hyperfocus in their jobs. They turn it into "the zone" and plan for intense concentration bouts. They take 10-minute breaks that give them time to do self-care habits or give the spouse or children some hugs. They set up their environment so there are no distractions and may have some music in the background. When they are in the zone, they are in a happy place conducive to health. Thus, being in the zone is healthy, whereas hyperfocus can be positive but doesn't equal being in the zone.

Hyperfocus abilities make it difficult to diagnose ADHD. If a child uses hyperfocus to study, they do well in school. And most kids with ADHD aren't necessarily good at school – although some are.

The big key about hyperfocus is the type of activities it's used for. If it's positive ones, and there is no health compromise, then hyperfocus is actually good. But to improve it, strive to be "in the zone."

When you decide to change hyperfocus into something for the good – or progress to being "in the zone," counseling may help.

Some of the questions posed during coaching include:

- How has hyperfocus helped you?
- How has it been a disadvantage to you?
- How can you harness it to your advantage?
- How can you break up intense periods of hyperfocus and include some socialization?
- What activities are your ADHD children hyperfocused on?

By limiting the time spent on hyperfocus activities and putting boundaries on the activity, such as when it can and can't be done, you gain control over hyperfocus.

REFLECTIONS

Time blindness and hyperfocus are behaviors that are common in ADHD. Unfortunately, they can interfere with you being unstoppable. The good news is that these are greatly improved with counseling and some behavior changes and tweaks. The ADHD tax hits those with

ADHD hard when they find out all the financial harm that their brain has caused. However, knowing the ADHD tax that one has paid is motivating for you to change. Just knowing you will make $1 million less than those who are neurotypical makes you think twice about not changing!

BIG CONCEPTS IN THIS CHAPTER

Here's a list of the big concepts for this chapter:

- Procrastination = avoidance of tasks or decisions
- ADHD tax = money lost because of ADHD symptoms
- Hyperfocus = so involved in what you like to do you lose track of time

In the next chapter, you'll learn even more about the beauty of your brain. It's a great chapter that will cause a paradigm change!

6

THE BEAUTY OF YOUR BRAIN

"I'm not crazy. I prefer the term mentally hilarious."

— ANONYMOUS

Your individuality is something to be happy about. It can even offer you a sense of pride. But once you start thinking about some of your little quirks, it can be downright funny! Think of that last burst of creativity you had where maybe you told your friends your out-of-the-box solution to stop crime. And remember how tense the room was at home after something happened until you broke the ice with a joke?

You aren't crazy. Your individuality needs to be experienced! There's humor and richness in the way your brain thinks.

ADHD can't be all bad. It could be associated with a life where success is possible. Think about Michael Phelps, the swimmer; Karina Smirnoff, the ballroom dancer; and Terry Bradshaw, who made it to the NFL Hall of Fame. And then there's Channing Tatum, the actor; Adam Levine, the musician; and even Richard Branson, the entrepreneur. Their ADHD didn't stop their progress and walked purposefully into their unstoppable-ness and resilience.

So, how are the brains of the neurodiverse differ from those who are neurotypical? That's what you'll learn in this chapter.

THE SCIENCE BEHIND THE ADHD BRAIN

In the 1960s, health practitioners used to teach children with ADHD that they had to slow down. They tried to get those with ADHD to use self-control methods that were taught to children with other neurological disorders. The problem was that they didn't work. For example, they would make children sit down and then read visualization exercises to them, encouraging them to change how hot the thermostat in their brain was working.

Then, more knowledge came forward. Imaging studies of the brain started showing what was really happening in the brain. Computed tomography (CT) and magnetic resonance imaging (MRI) were used to measure how large different parts of the brain were and how much volume they took up.

Electroencephalography (EEG) and SPECT (single-photon emission computed tomography) scans gave doctors information about nerve activity and blood flow.

Then, radioactive tracers with raclopride, which attached to dopamine receptors, were used for positron emission tomography (PET) scans. These scans showed scientists that dopamine levels were low in those with ADHD and that ADHD stimulant medications brought dopamine levels to normal about an hour after they were taken.

Functional scans were also done. These scans tell how well certain areas of a brain are working before and after an activity. These types of scans have a small letter f before the abbreviation of the scan. For example, fMRI means functional MRI, which shows how much oxygen is taken in by brain areas receiving a lot of nerve input.

Another scan, fMRI-DTI (an MRI with diffusion tensor imaging), measures the amount of crosstalk between different areas of the brain. Crosstalk should always be high, as all areas of the brain should constantly be communicating with each other. Still, in those with ADHD, crosstalk is significantly less.

Functional scans do have a disadvantage, though. They only consider the task during the exam but not other situations.

126 | ISABELLE RAY

All these types of brain imaging are helpful to understand the brain wiring in those with ADHD. Once the neuroimaging studies reveal any structural difference, it can explain why someone with ADHD has the symptoms they have.

WHY ADHD PEOPLE ARE WIRED DIFFERENTLY

There's a consensus among scientists that when the structural anatomy of the brain shows a smaller prefrontal cortex and basal ganglia – for example, which is seen in ADHD – focus and attention become a problem. That's when the behaviors seen in those with ADHD become likely. The behaviors aren't really choices the person is making – the behaviors result because of the structure of the brain.

One study compared 49 adults diagnosed with ADHD to 34 adults without ADHD. All of them were young adults around 16 years old. The researchers found differences in brain structure with these types of imaging studies. The young adults with ADHD were ones that no longer "qualified" for a diagnosis of ADHD in some cases. Still, nonetheless, they all had reduced brain volume. Decreased brain volume will potentially cause poor memory.

The scientists also found a miniaturized caudate nucleus area inside the gray matter. This is important for cognitive functions and memory. Those who did not have ADHD did not have these changes.

This study, done at universities in Cambridge, England, and Oulu, Finland, tells us that the 25 to 30 percent of adults who don't meet the diagnostic criteria for ADHD as they become adults really are not outgrowing their ADHD. Their brain structure is likely to not change – and it brings the functional impairments into their adult life.

But is brain structure fixed permanently, or can it change? To what extent do life habits play in this? If Dr. Amen finds that a protocol of nutrients can fix "holes" that appear on SPECT scans, then isn't that proof that the brain is one more part of the body that can heal when given the right circumstances?

There's a concept called neuroplasticity in neurology that you may already be familiar with. Neuroplasticity is the idea that your brain is ever-changing and adapting to your environment. If parts of the brain are not working as they should, other parts can learn to pick up the slack with different activities.

This means that by doing different activities or learning new skills, the brain of someone with ADHD can learn new ways of doing tasks that are not currently done correctly. It's similar to when someone has a heart attack – the blood vessels jump up to the new task to get the part of the heart that did not receive the blood flow and build a new route, compensating.

ADHD BRAIN VS. NON-ADHD BRAIN

For example, in those without ADHD, meditation for eight weeks alters the posterior cingulate area, which is used for self-awareness and when the mind is wandering. It also changes the left hippocampus, one of the areas used for cognition, memory, learning, and emotional regulation. When studies were done on those with ADHD, they saw similar changes.

The anterior cingulate cortex appears to also act differently in those with ADHD before and after a task. This area wasn't activated in brain scans, although it is activated and fully working in those without ADHD. This anterior cingulate cortex of the brain is essential for changing a person's focus and deciding how long the focus should be on that particular topic.

Because of neuroplasticity, those with ADHD had other areas of the brain that were working when the cognitive task was done. This confirms that for those with ADHD, it is hard to prioritize what to do and when. And it also affirms that neuroplasticity works.

There was another significant finding about the brains of those with ADHD. Even when the brain is "at rest," it's still working. Imaging studies have shown us that the regions of the brain that are still active – called the default mode network (DMN) – take care of mind-wandering, contemplation, and reflection.

These areas include the following:

- precuneus/posterior cingulate cortex – The precuneus area is involved in mental imagery strategies, reactivity to cues, perception of the environment, recollection and memory, how you feel when you have pain and the integration of information.
- medial prefrontal cortex
- lateral parietal cortex
- inferior parietal cortex

These areas are working when you are daydreaming, remembering things from the past, and considering what other people think and believe. These areas are not working when you are participating in acts of intention and goal-driven tasks. That's when pathways for attention start to work.

But in those with ADHD, the DMN forgets to turn off when the attention circuits are activated. It appears that the control center communication for the DMN needs to be boosted – and that's why someone with ADHD has lapses of attention.

An example is when someone with ADHD tells themselves it's time to pay bills, and the control center fails to signal the DMN to calm down. Then, a plate of cookies near the statements takes the person's attention, and the bills don't get paid, but the person feels satisfied with the cookies!

This dysfunction in the control pathways is the current theory scientists use to explain ADHD. The key is to strengthen those communication centers and improve the compensating areas. This is why different therapies make a big difference in the lives of those with ADHD.

However, it takes more than a pill to make a difference in someone with ADHD. And "a difference" means a reduction of symptoms by 40% or more. To patients, "a difference" means they are more organized, can work at their potential, or are less impulsive and more thoughtful.

Doctors have found that behavior therapies can't be done without medication and vice versa. Doing one without the other brings only about a 30% improvement.

A LIST OF THE DIFFERENCES IN THE BRAIN OF SOMEONE WITH ADHD

Here's a list of what scientists have found out about an ADHD brain:

- Total brain size smaller than normal
- Smaller brain volume in five subcortical areas
- Smaller amygdala (memory, emotion, and behavior regulation)
- Smaller hippocampus (memory, emotion, and behavior regulation)

- Smaller cerebellum (movement regulation)
- Decreased blood flow to prefrontal areas (the area responsible for executive functions)
- Dysfunctional brain connectivity between the frontal cortex of the brain and the visual processing area
- Dysregulation in two of the four pathways of the dopamine system related to cognitive functioning, such as the dopamine reward pathway, giving greater rewards than usual. The mesocortical pathway is also disrupted and is essential for executive functions such as working memory, cognition, and decision-making.
- Irregular blood flow in areas of the brain for cognitive, motor, and emotional regulation
- Default Mode Network (DMN) activity is active continually, leading to attention lapses
- Very high level of connectivity between brain regions that are related to the selective visual attention system (notice irrelevant things in the vision field.

LIST OF SKILLS PEOPLE WITH ADHD HAVE

Although every person with ADHD is unique, many people with ADHD have similar excellent traits. From the list below, you'll see that having ADHD could propel you to success in several different areas because these traits are not that common in the general population.

This list is based more on case studies of those with ADHD than actual studies. However, studies do show that those with ADHD have greater levels of creativity in not only art but also music, acting, mechanical tasks, and science.

1. Hyperfocus

The ability to focus on interesting tasks for hours at a time, tuning out everything else, is a distinct plus. It brings high-quality reports that are brilliant.

2. High energy

The high energy of those with ADHD makes them excellent at activities that engage their physical body. They tend to be good at sports.

3. Spontaneity and courage

Because those with ADHD tend to notice things that others don't, they are more spontaneous. They don't think about future ramifications or overthink situations and are likelier to go with a random idea than those without ADHD. They also turn impulsivity into spontaneity, which could mean being the life of a party. Often, spontaneity leads to lasting good memories.

Spontaneity also gives others the idea that they have greater amounts of courage. Spontaneity is unexpected in relationships, and it brings fun into the moment.

4. Great conversational skills

It's expected that those with ADHD are very talkative, and great conversationalists have higher levels of humor, social intelligence, and empathy. They also have a more positive attitude, which breeds more social success. Part of their success with conversations is they know how to reduce stress and cope with difficult situations. They bring humor into the situation. This helps them in romantic relationships, too.

5. Resilience

This skill is seen in about 50% of people with ADHD, but this percentage is changeable. If you are looking to improve your resilience and make efforts to do so, you will get what you seek.

Despite setbacks and much adversity, resilience means to keep plugging away, making progress. The resilience that is built in those with ADHD contributes to becoming a strong leader. This resilience is also seen in the makings of a deep self-awareness, which becomes a strength.

Part of their resilience may be because they are risk-takers. Failing 100 times at something doesn't mean they'll give up. They'll go out on a limb to take a risk and try something that hasn't been tried before. Those with ADHD persist.

6. Creativity

The creativity found in those with ADHD is often associated with excellent problem-solving ability because they think outside the box.

7. Positive Attitude

Perhaps it's because of all the challenges that those with ADHD are overcoming but a positive attitude is prevalent in them. They see the light at the end of the tunnel.

8. Generosity & Empathy

Those with ADHD can see into the lives of others and understand where they are coming from. That's why they are generous and empathetic. They also have a sense of fairness and have more profound compassion for others.

HOW THIS IS A STRENGTH

The benefits that those with ADHD have may be seen as superpowers. The boundless energy and ability to hyper-focus allow them to accomplish amazing things. Like Michael Jordan with ADHD, they can outlast other athletes on the playing field. The hyperfocus will enable them to screen out everything in their environment so that the sporting task at hand may be achieved.

The secret to making your ADHD superpowers shine is to build the skill you excel in, which will propel you to a position where that skill will be helpful and profitable. If you have a high IQ and can hyperfocus, you could write a book in a few weeks rather than months. Then, you could use your conversational skills to get it out into the world.

Of course, gauging the effects of your skills on others around you is essential, too. Some in the real world don't want to see that someone could write that book quickly while they struggle with their own book. Some prefer to be quiet rather than talk all the time. In behavior therapy, you'll learn how to handle these challenges.

For inspiration, here's a list of some people who have reported they have ADHD:

- Justin Timberlake, musician
- Ty Pennington, TV host
- Lisa Ling, journalist
- Glenn Beck, TV/radio personality
- Will Smith, actor
- Paris Hilton, business entrepreneur
- Jim Carrey, actor
- John Lennon, singer, songwriter
- George Bernard Shaw, playwriter
- Jules Verne, science fiction writer
- Walt Disney
- Wolfgang Amadeus Mozart, classical music composer

• Leonardo Da Vinci, artist

ADHD is highly manageable. The exceptional skills you are born with can be enhanced by medications and therapy. Hence, they help you reach the pinnacle of success. You can use these outstanding skills to be unstoppable.

FINDING YOUR FLOW

Your goal is really to find your flow. Doing this is easier than you may think!

WHAT IS FLOW STATE

Flow state, described in the national bestseller book Flow by Mihaly Csikszentmihalyi, is "an optimal state of consciousness where we feel our best and perform our best."

It's investing intense focus into a task that often results in brilliant work, such as books or art.

FLOW STATE VS. HYPERFOCUS

The flow state is considered optimal and healthy. Flow is intentional concentration, and it's disciplined. Hyperfocus is so intense that someone may go for hours without eating, drinking, or urinating. Hyperfocus occurs because of a lack of self-regulation. It can cause health issues over time. You can't depend on hyperfocus when you need to have it, and you can't self-induce or control it. But flow can be created.

THE BENEFITS OF FLOW STATE

Flow is one of your happy places. It's inside your mind, a place where you have the most self-acceptance, where you feel superhuman and like you are working on something that will improve humanity. When you're in this state, words come easy to you (or ideas if you are doing art), and there's virtually little stress or obstacles.

Flow allows you to continue doing what you are doing for hours – and it takes minimal effort. Your mind is stimulated at a very high level, and nothing else in your life competes for attention. When you have ADHD and feel a state of flow, you feel as if you have come face to face with the unbridled power of your mind.

HOW TO FIND YOUR FLOW

Below are some suggestions to turn on the flow!

1. Music helps to create a state of flow. Whatever music you choose should not be distracting.
2. You need an environment that is not distracting for a flow state.

138 | ISABELLE RAY

3. You need to be well-rested, well-fed (not overfed or underfed), well-hydrated, and with your kidneys and colon working well to stay in a flow state. Correct any of the habits associated with these before you start seeking flow. They all contribute.
4. You can't skip stimulant medication when attempting to get into a flow state.
5. Tell your closest friends and family members you plan on getting into a state of flow so they won't disrupt you and can hold you accountable.
6. Work in sprints of time that you determine (anywhere from 30 to 60 minutes usually). Take breaks in between that are under 10 minutes so your flow isn't lost. The breaks will allow you to integrate the work.
7. When you get thoughts and ideas running through your mind, enter them on a notepad. You can always go back to them later.
8. Keep a flow diary to find patterns of what worked the best and then repeat them.

HOW TO UNLOCK YOUR ADHD GIFTS USING THE FLOW STATE PSYCHOLOGY

The same qualities that promote flow also promote hyperfocus. That means that with ADHD, you can also enter into a state of flow. You may have an advantage over others to get to the state of flow!

Here are five guidelines.

1. Make sure the task is something you want to do. Getting into flow is more difficult if the task is not interesting, exciting, or on your "Yes, let me do this!" list.
2. Have a well-defined goal for your study period that leads to flow.
3. The task you do during the flow state must be challenging somehow.
4. What you do after a period of hyperfocus is not as compelling as what you do at other times. There are high dopamine rewards to being hyperfocused. Converting to something else that is lower in dopamine output is a transition. So, set a time limit for hyperfocus activities. Children may need an intermediary type of activity that transitions them from hyperfocus to chores. Whatever that is should be something fun. Don't fight hyperfocus. Harness it. Set up limits for it.
5. Think of ADHD as a specialist type of person in a community. The rest of the community may be generalists – and that's okay – but sooner or later, they will need a specialist. And that specialist is you, who comes to their rescue with creative solutions and hyperfocus sessions – or periods of flow – until you find an answer.

REFLECTIONS

By living with ADHD, you have a lot of skills and abilities that other non-ADHD people don't have. You have more compassion, empathy, resilience, creativity, spontaneity, and hyperfocus.

By honing them to your advantage, you can make it known that your superpowers are valuable. Learning how to turn hyperfocus into a flow state is beneficial in many ways. It turns your ADHD into an asset you may have never realized you had.

BIG CONCEPTS IN THIS CHAPTER

Here's a list of the big concepts for this chapter:

- Imaging studies showed us what was happening in the brain.
- Brains are wired differently in ADHD.
- Some parts of the ADHD brain are smaller and don't mature till later.
- DMN in an ADHD brain won't shut off during focus sessions.
- Fewer dopamine and serotonin receptors are found in those with ADHD.
- Connectivity between brain regions is different than in non-ADHD people.

- Skills in ADHD: hyperfocus, high energy, spontaneity, courage, conversational skills, resilience, creativity, positive attitude, generosity, empathy
- Successful ADHD people: Walt Disney, Justin Timberlake, Leonardo da Vinci
- Flow = optimal state of consciousness where you feel your best and perform your best

In the next chapter, you'll learn how self-care can improve your existence with ADHD.

7

STARTING WITH SELF-CARE

"No matter how you feel... Get up. Dress up. Show up. And don't give up."

— ANONYMOUS

This quote is appropriate for those with ADHD. It's all about the concept of resilience. Once you set up routines and structures that breed emotional stability, miracles begin to happen in your life.

Dealing with stress, social situations, and one's own emotions, as well as having enough food (at the correct times), water, sleep, and the right people in your life (who are emotionally stable), contribute significantly to resilience. Accepting one's diagnosis also is a big part of the picture.

144 | ISABELLE RAY

In this chapter, you'll learn much about all these. The result is you won't let situations or others define YOU. Resilience is a big part of being unstoppable.

ACCEPTING ADHD

Going through life thinking, "What's wrong with me? Why did I do that? Why am I like this? I didn't want to .... But I did ... anyway" happens a lot before you get your diagnosis of ADHD. This contributes to the suffering felt by those with ADHD. And it acts as a block to your forward progress.

Accepting your diagnosis of ADHD occurs the moment you realize you aren't broken, and your brain doesn't need fixing. It's the point where you discover you have ADHD, and ADHD doesn't have you. That's when the real you starts coming out bit by bit.

The process of finding yourself includes learning more about the condition and understanding what is happening neurologically. The more you know about ADHD, the better you understand why you approach problems differently and think differently. And that's why it's such a brilliant move for you to be reading this book.

IMPORTANCE OF ACCEPTING YOUR DIAGNOSIS

Your diagnosis helps you bridge the gap between your potential and what you didn't understand.

So far, you may feel like you are miles away from your potential. No matter what, there's a reason you are who you are. And that reason could be that even with all your weaknesses, you're the answer person in a room of people looking for answers. You're the one that gives off the light in the room; they aren't.

You're the one with the answer; they aren't. It's your conversation skills that fill a massive gap in relationships. There's something about you that when problems arise that people can't solve, you seem to quickly think outside the box and give the perfect solution.

When you accept your diagnosis, you acknowledge yourself. And that's when you begin to shine.

WHAT IT LOOKS LIKE TO ACCEPT YOUR ADHD

Despite everything happening in your family due to your ADHD, they still love you. Your drive is unequaled by others. Your hyperfocus brings brilliant solutions. Your sense of humor and empathy together are a blessing that would not exist if it wasn't for your ADHD. You are unique. And now you can love that.

Accepting your diagnosis means moving forward in life like you have not progressed. It means you can teach your children, students, and friends to accept who they are no matter what their diagnosis is. It means you have something to offer people – and you can see now that they are waiting for this.

It means you can live and spend time with yourself – and like it. It means you can listen to someone talk to you in a conversation but drop all the negative self-talk about how your response should be this or that. You realize that purely listening to someone uses a lot less energy than all the rest of that.

Accepting your diagnosis happens when you look at the advantages you have from ADHD and lose all the obstacles.

And accepting your diagnosis gives you the blessing of growing despite your ADHD. That's when you can see a direct outcome of what happens when what's happening neurologically is tweaked by you. That's when you start to see you aren't spaced out as much anymore, meet deadlines, and stay focused. It's a wow moment, for sure.

Accepting your diagnosis can also mean that you get knocked down by one of your behaviors again – but you get back up again and become resilient and unstoppable. You're tough and recover quickly. You face the stigma of what people believe about those with ADHD – and you still show up. You advocate for yourself and seek support.

You lead your life as best you can within a society of non-ADHD people.

WAYS/METHODS ON HOW TO ACCEPT YOUR DIAGNOSIS

The ways to accept your diagnosis all have to do with a reframe that occurs in your brain. The reframing is the same thing as a paradigm change.

Instead of thinking and focusing on all the negative things about ADHD, you shift your thoughts to a track where you focus on all the positive things.

Part of this may happen automatically on its own, but most people need some intervention. This can occur just from reading other people's stories or thoughts. Once you do this, the stigma is dropped from having the diagnosis of ADHD.

Below are some of them that will help in the shift:

- Instead of fixing yourself, just be yourself.
- Damaged? Nope, you're diverse instead.
- Your brain chemistry is just what it is – and you won't label it bad, broken, or related to something wrong with you.
- ADHD symptoms will still continue. But it's how you talk to yourself about what happened that will be different.

- ADHD is only one feature of who you are. All the rest of the features make up who you are.

BUILDING RESILIENCE AND SELF-ESTEEM

With a diagnosis of ADHD, you can start the process of finding out who you are. And suppose that diagnosis happens earlier when you are a child. In that case, it means you get the heads-up on how to build resilience and self-esteem much earlier than other children.

If you get the diagnosis of ADHD later in life, you can pick up all the pieces of your life and move ahead. For many people without ADHD, they never get the chance to do this.

Emotional dysregulation is a big part of ADHD. Anger outbursts, mood shifts, sensitivity, feelings of rejection, irritability, and other intense emotions may be a daily phenomenon.

But when you get the diagnosis, there's a shift in how all this must be considered. Instead of all of it being a significant stigma in your life, now it opens up an avenue to heal. And with each route you take to move forward, all that stigma starts to fall away simply because you're presenting another side of yourself to the world. You aren't your stigma anymore. You're building resilience and self-esteem.

The classes you'll take and the coaches you'll have will allow you to start practicing coping skills to achieve better emotional stability.

IMPORTANCE OF RESILIENCE

Building this resilience is one of the most important things you can do because of the alternate path that leads to anxiety, depression, trauma, and substance abuse. It's as if you have two possible choices in front of you: one of them is to get treatment, master emotional regulation, and build resilience. The other is to do nothing and experience more of what you've been experiencing in life up to this point and take it deeper toward substance abuse.

And remember that one-woman band from the beginning of the book? Well, the emotional coherence you get from choosing the path of emotional regulation allows you to harmonize all the instruments on the contraption and bring out a phenomenal melody.

The more aberrant signals you have – anxiety, depression, trauma, and all the associated physiological changes that go with them, the more the songs from the one-person band appear dissonant. The sound reverberates into others, keeping them away from you, not moving towards you. This only brings greater depths of frustration and disappointment to you.

Emotional regulation is also about healing your heart from past traumas. When left unhealed because of a lack of forgiveness, grudges, or resentment, these things become thorns in you that are continually interpreted in future situations as threats from others.

In reality, they reflect back to you alone, showing the status of your own heart. You expect to find trauma and find it even when it's nonexistent in a situation. Getting help for unresolved traumas becomes critical for those with ADHD, and it may be approached one of two ways – via regular or spiritual counseling.

HOW TO BE RESILIENT DESPITE YOUR ADHD

You'll learn how to be resilient in training classes or coaching, but here are the basic concepts.

Your Daily Habits

1. You can't achieve emotional resilience and stabilization if you don't eat right. Not eating regular meals or too many processed or sugary foods cause erratic changes in your blood sugar. As your blood sugar changes – going too high or too low, you lose regulation of your emotions. You'll experience anger outbursts, depression, anxiety, sweating, nervousness, headaches, dizziness, and fainting when blood sugars are not within the normal blood sugar zone. Until this

is fixed, there is no need to take any classes on emotional regulation because the methods simply will not work.

2. Lack of sleep and lack of exercise also will impair your emotional regulation.

3. Assess your habits of drinking alcohol and smoking. Make new decisions about them. Alcohol and smoking both affect your blood sugar levels, and when they do, they hijack your own control of your emotions in your body.

Proper Choice of Those to Help You on This Journey

1. Assess which are the healthy relationships in your life. You can't expect to get emotionally resilient if those around you are unhealthy. For example, hanging around hotheads only shows you how to be a hothead yourself. People imprint upon each other. Carefully choose who you will depend upon for the next six months to support and encourage you and who you will not. You don't have to ghost them all; explain that you're on an emotional sabbatical and will return in about six months, but you'll check in occasionally.

2. Psychotherapy in the form of cognitive behavioral therapy has the best track record for learning emotional stability. If choosing this route, you'll want to find out more details, such as how long the counselor has been

using it, how effectiveness is determined, and what type of homework is required.

3. Connect with groups on Facebook or elsewhere where everyone aims for the same sense of resilience. Everyone shares, no one condemns, and everyone benefits.

How to Deal with Stressors

1. When anyone with ADHD is overwhelmed, emotional outbursts will occur. For example, a child will have a temper tantrum. Adults will act differently depending on their personality; some still have temper tantrums!

What you do when exposed to stress will be critical to achieving daily emotional regulation. In many cultures, adaptogenic herbs such as ginseng or calming teas such as chamomile are taken to take the bite out of stressful situations. You might check with your doctor to see if it's okay for you to take any of these herbal aids.

2. Your plans to deal with stressors may also include shifting attention from the stressor, avoiding it, laughing or making jokes about it, mentally reframing a situation that is interpreted as deliberate harm to one that does not have evil intentions, and planning a step 1-2-3 of what to do with a newly found stressor.

3. Recount your little achievements along the way. You're good to go once you get a series of 5 or 6 wins in

emotional situations. Post them on your mirror to remind yourself that this can be achieved.

Personal Changes You May Have to Make

1. Drop the masking behaviors and open up about your vulnerability. It will make you authentic to others. Drop the negative self-talk. Practice the art of reframing. And keep moving forward no matter what.

2. Be compassionate with yourself when you screw up.

3. Give up perfectionism; it's too high a bar for anyone to strive for. Set more realistic tendencies.

4. Don't use force for your motivation; it won't work. Force sounds like "I have to do...." Compassion may be an alternative motivation if it fits the situation.

5. Stay on track with your resilience program. Review your progress weekly. Check your methods for staying on track. How did you counter the temptation of immediate gratification? How can you address any relapses? Do I need anything else, such as more support?

REFLECTIONS

Resilience is what every successful person with ADHD has built. Along with resilience comes a higher self-esteem. Resilience is made by changing the mind first, then changing the environment, and finally adding other effective, well-known strategies.

Know that the methods you use for building resilience identify and deactivate stress in your life. They will undoubtedly be used for the rest of your life. Stay on track with your resilience program. If you get off track, use self-compassion and analysis of what happened to get back on track. Moving forward is always your resilience goal.

BIG CONCEPTS IN THIS CHAPTER

Here's a list of the big concepts for this chapter:

- Accepting ADHD – you aren't broken
- Damaged? No, you're diverse.
- Resilience: Dump the sugar, irregular meals, lack of sleep/exercise, alcohol, smoking
- Do what it takes to become unstoppable
- Coming up next is understanding more about impulsivity.

8

UNDERSTANDING ADHD IMPULSIVITY: WHAT YOU NEED TO KNOW

> Before you make a decision, ask yourself this question: will you regret the results or rejoice in them?"
>
> — ROB LIANO

Impulsivity. It can be good, but more often than not, it isn't good. Hasty decisions with unforeseen consequences can ruin lives.

The quote by Rob Liano encourages introspection about the potential for future regrets. Is it possible to balance embracing new experiences and consider the long-term implications? You bet! Read this chapter and find out how.

WHAT IS IMPULSIVITY?

Impulsivity occurs in a situation when you can't inhibit behavioral impulses and thoughts.

Do you remember those brain studies that showed that different parts of the brain are not communicating with each other in those with ADHD?

One of the results of this lack of communication is impulsivity. Another is emotional dysregulation, and a third is inattention.

Impulsivity is seen in those with ADHD in the following ways:

- the student blurts out an answer before the teacher finishes the question
- someone reacts with yelling or a punch in the gut when frustrated
- someone splurges on fast food or chocolate
- someone lashes out at another with all types of sarcasm and hurtful words

These behaviors aren't supposed to happen because the thalamus is supposed to prevent them from happening. There are a few steps to this process:

1. The brain detects a situation that has to be handled.
2. The connections between the limbic system and the hippocampus send a warning to the frontal cortex via the thalamus.
3. The thalamus does not prevent the emotional expression and lets it go through.

This tells us that impulsivity is not occurring because someone is flat-out rude. It's not happening because the person cannot discipline their tongue. It's because of the signaling system inside the brain.

Impulsivity does not happen in ALL people with ADHD.

Impulsivity may be suitable for comedians, but it's not good for anyone else. We're expected to act appropriately in society. A punch in the gut can land someone in jail. An insult to someone will potentially result in the loss of friendships.

TRIGGERS THAT MAKE YOU IMPULSIVE

Identifying the triggers that make you jump into behaviors you may regret later is important.

Below is a list of some of them you may face daily:

- You're waiting in a long line. This can bring out the worst in some people!

- You're at a social networking event and really need to talk to someone talking to three other people. You can't wait till they stop talking.
- You're at a skate park, and some incredible skateboarders are showing off their skills.
- You're at a heated discussion in the neighborhood.
- You went to a drive-in, barely arrived in time, and are starving.
- Your parents have told you five times this week that you can't use the car.
- You're driving on an open stretch of road and are faced with the impulse to drive as fast as you can.

Journaling helps you identify these triggers. Just put your mind to it.

SIGNS OF IMPULSIVITY IN PEOPLE WITH ADHD

Below is a list of scenarios where impulsivity is occurring:

1. Someone acts out or speaks without thinking.
2. Without planning, somebody starts a new task.
3. Someone does something self-destructive and risky to their health or life.
4. Someone makes a big decision in the spur of the moment instead of thinking it through.
5. Someone interrupts another in a conversation.
6. Patience is almost nonexistent in a person.
7. Racing thoughts inside one's head are a problem.

8. Saving money for the future is just about impossible.

9. Someone is driving along a busy highway during rush hour.

10. Someone goes out to a nightclub to socialize but brings someone they don't know home with them.

WHAT TRIGGERS IMPULSIVITY IN PEOPLE WITH ADHD

The two neurotransmitters dopamine and serotonin play a role in impulsivity. Dopamine is the neurotransmitter that tells you to move forward with the action in your head. Serotonin tells you to stop.

This plays out in real life because when you get enough dopamine, you proceed with whatever you want. You have the motivation to do it. Then, serotonin tells you that you accomplished the task and makes you happy. When both work together, you don't make rash decisions.

However, both neurotransmitters can override each other.

Well, in ADHD, there's no balance between the two. ADHD usually has fewer dopamine receptors, and as a result, they don't get the go-ahead signal. This is why those with ADHD procrastinate and can't stay on task.

But there's more. Those with ADHD also have low numbers of serotonin receptors, so they can't resist an impulse.

A few studies have shown that when stimulation causes dopamine production, super-high amounts of dopamine are produced. That means an increase of impulses at a higher rate – and they overwhelm the already taxed serotonin receptors. The result is emotional escalation. And sudden, intense bursts of emotions trigger higher amounts of dopamine.

Journaling about past triggers of impulsivity will help you analyze how you could have acted differently in a situation. It enables you to avoid the same mistakes again and again. Your impulsivity could be buying chocolate ice cream and then eating the whole carton. In this case, journaling about it may uncover two triggers – one for purchasing the ice cream and another for eating it all in one sitting.

DIET IS LINKED TO IMPULSIVITY TRIGGERS

You may not have considered diet a source of impulsivity triggers, but it is.

Here are five examples:

- A zinc deficiency causes similar symptoms in ADHD, such as restlessness, inattentiveness, and delayed cognitive development. Although more studies have to be done, there is a correlation of low zinc levels in children with ADHD. Bring on the zinc!

- Stimulant medications also cause appetite suppression, which leads to taking in less nutrients than what they need. This makes getting the zinc – and other nutrients the brain needs nearly impossible.
- Food additives are also linked to ADHD symptoms such as impulsivity, inattention, and hyperactivity. Consuming foods with food additives can actually cause those same symptoms in children who do not have ADHD as well. Likewise, these can affect adults as well. Try adding the Yuka app to your phone which will help you make better choices for foods and cosmetics.
- One meta-study showed that about 8% of children with ADHD have symptoms of ADHD related to the consumption of artificial food colors. Many adults with ADHD have noticed similar associations.
- Stimulant medications can increase the incidence of sleep disturbances, which also triggers impulsive behavior. They frequently wake up during the night.

HOW TO CONTROL IMPULSIVE BEHAVIOR

When there's impulsive behavior, it's as if there will be negative consequences if one doesn't do that behavior right now. "Just go for it" is the motto, and it's fueled by a push from somewhere inside the brain. The person feels like they will 'die' if they don't do it.

They don't think about whether or not the idea is good or bad until after they do it.

The problem is that guilt and regret are the results if these impulses are self-destructive.

STRATEGIES ON HOW TO MANAGE AND CONTROL IMPULSIVE BEHAVIOR

Here's what has been found about managing this type of behavior.

1. Regular exercise

About 30 minutes of aerobic exercise daily reduces ADHD symptoms, including impulsivity. The exercise lessens the intensity of the impulses.

2. Try delaying the impulse

Tell yourself that you'll wait a little while before you act on it. During the delay, you can decide if it's worth indulging in. For example, you get an impulse to purchase $400 worth of new clothes online. By telling yourself you will keep this option open but wait a few days to collect opinions on which dresses would look best on you, you will find that the impulse is much less intense – and you may even pass it up altogether.

3. **Make it more challenging to do the impulsive behavior.**

This complicates the task – which your ADHD brain hates!

For example, you could tell yourself you can have chocolate ice cream, but you'll have to return to the store only after you eat a good meal. Or you could make yourself take notes at a meeting and leave a section for questions you have a strong desire to ask.

4. **Train yourself on recognizing good, healthy impulses. Show yourself compassion in the process.**

This is best done with your diary. The analysis process is your training, and you'll begin doing more positive than negative ones. And the self-discovery along the way makes you feel brilliant!

5. **Participate in impulsive sports like gymnastics or tennis.**

These are generally reactive sports, and you can also participate in arts and crafts and role-playing games where you make on-the-spot decisions. These are ways to embrace your impulsive behaviors, which may result in teaching yourself that there's a time and place for them.

6. **Cognitive behavioral therapy and mindfulness (meditation or breathing exercises) training are helpful, as are ADHD medications.**

Learning emotional management skills will also help.

7. **Remove triggers of impulsivity.**

Determine the environments that contribute to these triggers.

REFLECTIONS

Managing impulsivity is something you can do. You can identify the triggers, adjust your daily routines, and get training and/or counseling for about six months. This will give you enough time to get a handle on it.

Once you get to a point where you feel like there's been a significant change in your impulsivity, you'll feel as if your ADHD is controllable. You'll be empowered – and unstoppable!

BIG CONCEPTS IN THIS CHAPTER

Here's a list of the big concepts for this chapter:

- Impulsivity: inability to inhibit behavioral impulses and thoughts
- Triggers contribute to impulsivity.
- Triggers are related to dopamine and serotonin receptors.
- Diet is linked to impulsivity triggers.
- Manage and control impulsive behavior with exercise, delaying the impulse, making it more challenging to do the behavior, cognitive behavioral therapy, breathing exercises, removing triggers.

In the next chapter, you'll learn about the role that emotions have in your ADHD.

9

THE CONNECTION BETWEEN YOU AND YOUR EMOTIONS

"Living with ADHD is like walking up a down escalator. You can get there eventually, but the journey is exhausting."

— KATHLEEN ELY

The journey is exhausting primarily because of intense emotional outbursts. These use up a lot of mental and physical energy. Then there's also the additional energy it takes to accomplish tasks that come much more quickly to others. And the persistence, resilience, and struggle to keep up with the constant challenges. The whole journey is like striving against an invisible current.

WHAT IS EMOTIONAL DYSREGULATION?

Emotional regulation is required to live with other people. Weeks won't go by when someone doesn't say something that can make anyone angry or do something that sets off an alarm in your head. One of the most common things to happen is the notorious toothpaste tube that is squeezed in the middle versus rolled up! Yet, we must act in ways that preserve relationships, forgive, and move forward to the next day.

When you learn emotional regulation, your moods are stable. You can work on teams, in partnerships, in a marriage, with larger people groups, and with communities. But suppose you are temperamental or exceptionally sensitive. In that case, you experience marked mood swings, unstable moods, and overly intense emotions. You're out of control. Your chances of advancing in a career are low, just as your chances of experiencing continual stress are high.

The more problems you have with emotional dysregulation, the more others feel like they can't be themselves around you. And the more you overreact, the more likely you'll conclude that you can't trust your own emotions.

WHAT IS EMOTIONAL DYSREGULATION?

Emotional dysregulation is the inability to control your emotions in different situations or what's happening to you internally. The result is exaggerated reactions that don't match the situation. Some people with ADHD have reported that their emotions often feel like they are either at a 0 or 100 on a score where 0 is no emotions, and 100 is the highest level of emotions that can be felt.

CAUSES OF EMOTIONAL DYSREGULATION

Besides ADHD as a cause of emotional dysregulation, there are other reasons it happens. For example, traumatic events during very early childhood could cause it because the events are so traumatic that they disrupt the brain during its development. Fetal alcohol syndrome and child abuse may also be culprits. There's neglect and abuse whenever a child does not have his needs met for safety, emotions, social, physical, housing, health, and clothing.

A traumatic brain injury from a fall where the head is hit or a blow to the head from any reason and continual rejection, criticism, or being ignored, which invalidates someone, are also possible reasons for emotional dysregulation occurring.

Certain mental disorders or brain disorders are also considered causes of emotional dysregulation. This includes PTSD (post-traumatic stress disorder), autism, obsessive-compulsive disorder, borderline personality disorder, and frontal lobe disorders.

SIGNS AND SYMPTOMS OF EMOTIONAL DYSREGULATION

There are many different signs and symptoms to look for regarding emotional dysregulation. Once you read through the list, you'll understand why they are on this list.

Here's the list:

Psychological issues:

- Anxiety
- Depression
- Shame
- Excessive fear
- Suicidal thoughts or threats
- Extreme perfectionism
- Sudden outbursts of anger
- Difficulty calming down after intense emotions
- Very little tolerance for frustration or being annoyed
- Anger
- Holding grudges longer than you should
- Refocusing attention away from emotions is difficult
- Trouble resolving conflict
- Emotional reactions seem to be too great for their cause

- Feeling completely overwhelmed by one's emotions
- Accusatory statements

Additional issues:

- Trouble sleeping
- Exaggerated crying fits
- Self-harm
- Substance use
- High-risk sexual behaviors
- Eating disorders
- Interpersonal relationships conflict

If emotional dysregulation occurs in children, they may be defiant, have few friends, don't want to comply with parents or teachers, and can't focus on tasks.

STEPS, METHODS, AND WAYS ON HOW TO DEAL AND COPE WITH EMOTIONAL DYSREGULATION

When you're ready to deal with emotional dysregulation, there are a few things to consider –

1) what do you do to prevent it from happening again

2) what do you do when it's actually happening.

You'll need both to gain the emotional regulation you seek.

Dealing with Mood Swings and Emotional Dysregulation

Like impulsivity, dealing with mood swings and emotional dysregulation should start with a healthy diet, meal timing, sleep, and exercise routines. Once these are in place, there will be fewer stress reactions to what's occurring.

WHAT TO DO BEFORE THE NEXT EMOTIONAL DYSREGULATION INCIDENT OCCURS

Emotional dysregulation can catch us off guard. In fact, that's why it's important to have a proactive plan in place.

Here are some practical strategies to help us prepare for these times and maintain a sense of balance:

1. List Your Coping Behaviors

Make a list of how you can cope healthily. Don't depend on only one coping mechanism. Post your list on the fridge so you can access the list quickly and have another list in your car and purse.

2. Be Like Abe Lincoln

Abe Lincoln tackled his bad habits and behaviors one at a time. Every month, he worked on one bad habit or behavior until he developed the neurological pathways in his brain to overcome it. Act like Abe. Start out by doing some soul-searching about your life, especially looking for areas where you can improve.

3. Antidepressant Medications or Antipsychotic Medications

Discuss this with your doctor or psychologist. You may find answers.

4. Counseling

One type is called dialectical behavior therapy (DBT). This therapy teaches patients how to become aware of what they think and feel, stay present, and deal with stress. DBT counselors categorize different states of mind as a reasonable mind (uses logic), an emotional mind (uses emotions, sensations, and moods), or a wise mind (a combination of both of them). This therapy's goal is better emotional management by combining emotions and logic.

5. Learn All About Emotional Dysregulation

If your child has ADHD, classes on how to cope with their emotional dysregulation will decrease your learning curve on how to deal with it. One of the strategies offered in these classes is that being calm makes a big difference.

WHAT CAUSES RAPID MOOD SWINGS IN WOMEN WITH ADHD

There are two possible reasons why emotional dysregulation occurs in those with ADHD:

1. The amygdala is overactive.
2. The frontal cortex is underactive.

The amygdala's function is to trigger normal emotions in response to internal and external situations. When the amygdala is overactive, then feelings are magnified.

The function of the frontal cortex is to filter and inhibit emotions so you can react civilly. For example, someone aggravates you, but you stay friendly and polite so the situation doesn't worsen. On the other hand, when the cortex is not working as it should – underactive – it doesn't prevent those emotional reactions from occurring.

Explosive tempers and impulsive behavior result from an overactive amygdala and an underactive frontal cortex. And some scientists say it's because the connection between the cerebral cortex and the amygdala is weak.

HOW ADHD AMPLIFIES EMOTIONAL DYSREGULATION

Emotional regulation has five components to it:

- recognizing your own emotions
- recognizing emotions in other people
- emotional reactivity (how much emotion can you handle, for how long before you react to it)
- the ability to calm yourself down
- the ability to improve your mood

One study analyzed 77 different studies on emotional regulation in children with ADHD and found they had the most difficulty with emotional reactivity, calming themselves down, and changing their mood.

Those with ADHD feel emotions at a higher intensity than non-ADHD people. And it's estimated that over two-thirds – 70% of those with ADHD have difficulty regulating their emotions. Another study of 61 children with ADHD reported that there may be a pattern of emotional dysregulation that happens when symptoms of ADHD occur.

HOW TO MANAGE RAPID MOOD SWINGS BROUGHT BY ADHD

WHAT CAN YOU DO RIGHT NOW WHEN YOU FEEL OVERLY INTENSE EMOTIONS ARE COMING UPON YOU?

1. When feeling a strong negative feeling, identify it and what caused it. Is it anger? Anxiety? Depression? Sadness? Frustration? Shame? This helps you understand it better.

Then, identify any signs of these emotions occurring in your body, such as a headache, stomachache, worry, or anxiety. This helps you create distance between body responses and feelings.

Diary about the incident. This helps you problem solve and gain insight about what's happening. You'll include your thoughts during the situation, how the thoughts made you feel, and the consequences.

2. Exercise instead of reacting. A walk or run around the block does wonders to change your moods.

3. Listen to music or play a musical instrument.

4. Utilize deep breathing exercises to calm yourself or your child. It's impossible to have hot emotions unless the breath rate is high. Once you start taking deep breaths, the entire body relaxes, and so do the feelings.

5. Consider trying flower remedies. One of the most popular ones on the market is the Bach Flower Emergency Rescue formula. It's a significantly diluted essence of flowers used specifically for emotional upheavals. Many people state nothing works faster! Do some research on them; they do not interfere with medications.

REFLECTIONS

Emotional regulation is your goal if you or your child has ADHD. Emotional dysregulation is wearing on the mind, body, and soul. It should be handled in two ways: by learning the ropes via classes, coaches, and counselors and by having strategies ready to go as soon as possible. Both of them together will work. And that's when you'll feel emotionally stable.

Emotional stability is one of the most essential skills to have in life. Once you master this, stressful situations are easy to go through, relationships become easy to navigate, and personal goals are easy to complete. It's a big key to your unstoppability.

BIG CONCEPTS IN THIS CHAPTER

Here's a list of the big concepts for this chapter:

- Emotional Dysregulation: inability to control your emotions
- Causes: trauma as a child, fetal alcohol syndrome, child abuse, ADHD, PTSD, autism
- Coping with emotional dysregulation: analyze preventive steps and create a plan of what to do when it happens.
- Parents – become emotionally regulated yourself first before working on the child.
- Rapid mood swings from overactive amygdala and underactive frontal cortex.

CONCLUSION

You have just learned more about your brain and how it works by reading this book than most people in their entire lifetime, even those who don't have a diagnosis of ADHD.

You've confronted behaviors that your brain orchestrates on an unconscious level and met them head-on with courage, introspection, and a resolute spirit. It takes remarkable fortitude to confront these challenges, and you've proven yourself to be nothing short of extraordinary.

In your pursuit of understanding, you have gained profound insights into your unique situation, insights that may have otherwise eluded you. Learning about ADHD and how the ADHD brain is wired is the pivotal first step towards reshaping your life, and you've already taken it.

You know grasp that having a challenge, such as ADHD, need not dictate the course of your life. As you've discovered, you were born and sculpted with a formidable arsenal of strengths that render you unstoppable: hyperfocus, boundless energy, spontaneity, courage, adept conversational skills, resilience, creativity, a positive attitude, generosity, and empathy. That's an impressive ten, and there are likely another ten to this list.

What Your Future Holds

Your journey forward may involve 'll ADHD medication, behavioral therapy, nutrition and dietary adjustments, coaching, counseling, and not the least, the unwavering support of your loved ones. It's about harnessing your ADHD brain – directing it, training it, and compelling it to align with your goals and aspirations. This is how an ADHD brain transforms into your greatest asset, how you become an unstoppable force, cultivating resilience, leadership, and great depth of character. These qualities empower you to achieve your goals and unlock latent potentials – of which you possess many!

Gone are the days when you lived in a void, grappling with the enigma of your actions or words, often baffled by your own choices. Procrastination will soon be a relic of the past, masking less frequent, and time blindness will yield to heightened time sensitivity. The ADHD tax is quickly dwindling, for you are now wise to its encumbrance.

The era of self-condemnation, where you shouldered the blame for the discord orchestrated by your one-person band, is behind you. Ahead lie days of emotional regulation, the pleasures of deliberate hyperfocus and being in the zone, fulfilling relationships with friends and family, and productive, awe-inspiring moments that will not only astonish yourself but also those fortunate enough to witness them. Embrace these days wholeheartedly!

The Opportunity Unfolds

Armed with the knowledge and tools at your disposal, your ADHD diagnosis transforms into an opportunity to maximize your strengths while mastering your vulnerabilities. Small, incremental changes can wield substantial influence over how you navigate life with ADHD. With these strategies, you can assert greater control over your life, enhance your overall well-being, and lead a more fulfilling life.

You are Unstoppable and Resilient!

Yet, above all else, remember: You are genuinely unstoppable! This unwavering belief will sustain you will through the learning curve and usher you into a future teeming with prosperity across your work, education, family life, health, and relationships.

So, go forth now – strike up the most enchanting melodies on your one-woman band, those pleasant melodies that turn everyone's head, induce heartfelt smiles, and transform the world. It's your destiny!

May I ask for a favor? Would you consider leaving a review on Amazon or wherever you purchased this book? Your review could serve as a guiding light for others embarking on their journey to conquer ADHD, paying it forward by offering them an invaluable head start on their path to transformation.

BIBLIOGRAPHY

References-Chp. 1

Abel EL. Prenatal effects of alcohol. Drug Alcohol Depend 1984 Sep;14(1):1-10.https://pubmed.ncbi.nlm.nih.gov/6386408/

Franz AP, et al. Attention-deficit/hyperactivity disorder and very preterm/very low birth weight: a meta-analysis. Pediatrics 2018 Jan;141(1):e20171645. https://pubmed.ncbi.nlm.nih.gov/29255083/

Glass L, et al. Neuropsychological deficits associated with heavy prenatal alcohol exposure are not exacerbated by ADHD. Neuropsychology 2013 Nov;27(6):713-24.https://pubmed.ncbi.nlm.nih.gov/24040921/

Hinshaw SP, et al. Annual Research Review: Attention-deficit/hyperactivity disorder in girls and women: underrepresentation, longitudinal processes, and key directions. J Child Psychol Psychiatry. 2022 Apr;63(4):484-496. https://pubmed.ncbi.nlm.nih.gov/34231220/

Porter MSM, et al. Low-moderate prenatal alcohol exposure and offspring attention-deficit hyperactivity disorder (ADHD): systematic review and meta-analysis. Arch Gynecol Obstet 2019 Aug;300(2):269-277.https://pubmed.ncbi.nlm.nih.gov/31161393/

Sciberras E, et al. Prenatal risk factors and the etiology of ADHD – review of existing evidence. Curr Psychiatry Rep 2017 Jan;19(1):1.https://pubmed.ncbi.nlm.nih.gov/28091799/

TEDxTalks. The most important lesson from 83,000 brain scans. Daniel Amen. TEDxOrangeCoast. 9 years ago. Accessed Aug. 16, 2023. https://youtu.be/esPRsT-lmw8

https://www.amenclinics.com/conditions/adhd-add/#:~:text=Type%207%3A%20Anxious%20ADD,be%20magnified%20by%20their%20anxiety

References-Chp. 3

Barth C., et al. Sex hormones affect neurotransmitters and shape the adult female brain during hormonal transition periods. Front

Neurosci 2015;9:37.https://www.ncbi.nlm.nih.gov/pmc/articles/PMC4335177/

Dorani F, et al. Prevalence of hormone-related mood disorder symptoms in women with ADHD. J Psychiatr Res 2021 Jan;133:10-15. https://pubmed.ncbi.nlm.nih.gov/33302160/

Konikowska K, et al. The influence of components of diet on the symptoms of ADHD in children. Rocz Panstw Zaki Hig 2012;63(2):127-34. https://pubmed.ncbi.nlm.nih.gov/22928358/

https://pubmed.ncbi.nlm.nih.gov/33307923/

https://www.northvalleywomenscare.com/blog/4-essential-vitamins-for-hormonal-imbalance

https://www.ncbi.nlm.nih.gov/pmc/articles/PMC6366354/

References- Chp. 5

Carrer LRJ.Music and sound in time processing of children with ADHD. Front Psychiatry. 2015;6:127. doi:10.3389/fpsyt.2015.00127

Niermann HCM, Scheres A. The relation between procrastination and symptoms of attention-deficit hyperactivity disorder (ADHD) in undergraduate students. Int J Methods Psychiatr Res 2014 Dec; 23(4): 411-421.https://www.ncbi.nlm.nih.gov/pmc/articles/PMC6878228/

Nazari MA, Mirloo MM, Rezaei M, Soltanlou M.Emotional stimuli facilitate time perception in children with attention-deficit/hyperactivity disorder. J Neuropsychol. 2018;12(2):165-175. doi:10.1111/jnp.12111

Rubia K.Cognitive neuroscience of attention deficit hyperactivity disorder (ADHD) and its clinical translation. Front Hum Neurosci. 2018;0. doi:10.3389/fnhum.2018.00100

https://www.verywellmind.com/what-is-dopamine-5185621

https://adhdtraction.com/the-adhd-tax/

References-Chp. 6

https://www.additudemag.com/current-research-on-adhd-breakdown-of-the-adhd-brain/#:~:text=The%20ADHD%20Brain%3A%20Structurally%20Different&text=Several%20studies%20have%20pointed-ed%20to,a%20difference%20in%20behavioral%20preference

Famous People with ADHD: ADD Celebrities and Well Known People.

April 15, 2021 updated. Mentalup.co https://www.mentalup.-co/blog/famous-people-and-celebrities-with-adhd Accessed Sept. 18, 2023.

References- Chp. 8

Monopoli WJ, Evans SW, Benson K, et al. Assessment of a conceptually informed measure of emotion dysregulation: Evidence of construct validity vis a vis impulsivity and internalizing symptoms in adolescents with ADHD. *Int J Methods Psychiatr Res.* 2020;29(4):1-14. doi:10.1002/mpr.1826

Buckholtz JW, Treadway MT, Cowan RL, et al.Dopaminergic network differences in human impulsivity. *Science.* 2010;329(5991):532-532. doi:10.1126/science.1185778

Waldera R, Deutsch J.Adhd and physical activity. *TPE.* 2021;78(6). doi:10.18666/TPE-2021-V78-I6-10563

Bioch, MH, Mulqueen J. Nutritional supplements for the treatment of attention-deficit hyperactivity disorder. Child Adolesc Psychiatr Clin N Am 2014 Oct;23(4):883-897.

Arnold LE, Lofthouse N, and Hurt E. Artificial food colors and attention-deficit/hyperactivity symptoms: conclusions to dye for. Neurotherapeutics 2012 Jul;9(3):599-609.

Nigg JT, et al. Meta-analysis of attention-deficit/hyperactivity disorder or attention-deficit/hyperactivity disorder symptoms, restriction diet, and synthetic food color additives. J Am Acad Child Adolesc Psychiatry 2012 Jan;51(1):86-97.

References- Chp. 9

Graziano PA, Garcia A. Attention-deficit hyperactivity disorder and children's emotion dysregulation: A meta-analysis. *Clinical Psychology Review.* 2016;46:106-123. doi:10.1016/j.cpr.2016.04.011

Beheshti A, et al. Emotion dysregulation in adults with attention deficit hyperactivity disorder: a meta-analysis. BMC Psychiatry 20, Mar 2020.https://bmcpsychiatry.biomedcentral.com/articles/10.1186/s12888-020-2442-7

Tate M, Greenberg DM, O'Neill S.Sound and feeling: Musical training moderates the association between adult ADHD and emotion regulation. In: *Future Directions of Music Cognition*. The Ohio State University Libraries; 2021. doi:10.18061/FDMC.2021.0024

Zimmermann MB, Diers K, Strunz L,Scherbaum N, Mette C. Listening to Mozart improves current mood in adult adhd – a randomized controlled pilot study. *Front Psychol.* 2019;10:1104. doi:10.3389/fpsyg.2019.01104

McQuade JD and Breaux RP. Are elevations in ADHD symptoms associated with physiological reactivity and emotion dysregulation in children? Journal of Abnormal Child Psychology 45, 2017: 1091-1103.

Made in the USA
Monee, IL
07 March 2025

13617280R00105